Choosing Your Career, Finding Your Vocation

 *Integration Books*

STUDIES IN PASTORAL PSYCHOLOGY, THEOLOGY, AND SPIRITUALITY
Robert J. Wicks, General Editor

also in this series

Clinical Handbook of Pastoral Counseling
edited by R. Wicks, R. Parsons, and D. Capps
Adolescents in Turmoil, Parents Under Stress
by Richard D. Parsons
Pastoral Marital Therapy
by Stephen Treat and Larry Hof
The Art of Clinical Supervision
edited by B. Estadt, J. Compton and M. Blanchette
The Art of Passingover
by Francis Dorff, O. Praem
Losses in Later Life
by R. Scott Sullender
Pastoral Care Emergencies
by David K. Switzer
Spirituality and Personal Maturity
by Joann Wolski Conn

Choosing Your Career, Finding Your Vocation

A Step by Step Guide for Adults and Counselors

Roy Lewis

Integration Books
paulist press/new york and mahwah

Copyright © 1989 by Roy Lewis

All rights reserved. No part of this book may be reproduced or transmitted in any form or by any means, electronic or mechanical, including photocopying, recording or by any information storage and retrieval system without permission in writing from the Publisher.

Library of Congress Cataloging-in-Publication Data

Lewis, Roy, 1937–
    Choosing your career, finding your vocation: a step by step guide for adults and counselors/Roy Lewis.
    p. cm.—(Integration books)
  Bibliography: p.
  ISBN 0-8091-3099-8
  1. Pastoral counseling. 2. Vocational guidance. 3. Vocation.
I. Title. II. Series.
BV4012.2.L49   1989
253.5—dc20   89-33658
                                                                         CIP

Published by Paulist Press
997 Macarthur Boulevard
Mahwah, New Jersey 07430

Printed and bound in the
United States of America

Contents

Foreword by Dr. Robert J. Wicks 1

Introduction 3

1. Our Human Resources 7
2. God and Vocation 30
3. Getting Started 52
4. Vocational Targeting 75
5. Career Development 99
6. The Dual Career Family 125

Notes 145

Foreword

Choosing Your Career, Finding Your Vocation evolves out of a belief by Roy Lewis that "People make career choices not at a single isolated moment, but out of the ongoing context of a lifetime of experiences." The dynamic process of career development is presented by him, then, as the result of an interaction of many forces, needs, and challenges.

In this readable and practical work, Lewis not only brings to the fore information which is not readily available, but, of even greater import, he raises our awareness of God's part in our occupational life.

Although this book provides good coverage of the concepts of adult career development, one of its most helpful features is the clarity with which Lewis also addresses the practical issues involved in "getting started" through needs assessment, data gathering, evaluation of career options, and planning and execution of the vocational search. In addition to this information, he provides essential information on "career development" and "the dual career family."

Choosing Your Career, Finding Your Vocation by Roy Lewis is a useful book not only for pastoral ministers/counselors, but especially for those seeking to see how their present and future career choices can become more fully part of God's plan for them and the community within which they live, work and worship. Work has always been an important part of life. This book aids all who read it to understand more fully how to make choices that will foster not only a sense of career, but also a sense of vocation. Given this point, I think it will be easy for you to see why I feel Roy Lewis' book is a real gift to both persons seeking guidance in career development and the ministers and counselors who assist them.

Robert J. Wicks
Series Editor

Introduction

Work is a major part of human experience. Many people spend more time at work than at any other activity, except perhaps sleep. Everyone works at something. Work is one of the major sources of satisfaction and dissatisfaction in adult life. It is central to most people's daily existence and affects their entire outlook and life-style. Freud astutely observed that work and love, *arbeiten* and *lieben*, are the hallmarks of maturity. People need to engage in satisfying work activities and meaningful love relationships.

The old question rings in our ears, "What will you do when you grow up?" As a grown-up, we are supposed to know what work to do. As adults we expect to be engaged in meaningful and satisfying work. For many adults, however, it is not that simple. Very few of us know what we want to do when we leave high school or even college. Yes, we work at a "job" that brings money. We become involved in some work because that's expected, but most of us wander around in our work life seeking that right occupation or career for ourselves. Most adults change occupation four to five times during their adult life.

Career counseling, known by various and sundry rubrics such as vocational guidance, occupational counseling, vocational counseling, proceeds through a well established body of knowledge and techniques to assist persons in choosing meaningful, reasonable and satisfying careers.

Most career historians single out Frank Parsons as the individual who first formulated vocational guidance. In his book, *Choosing a Vocation*, published in 1909, he clearly stated that a wise choice of vocation involved three factors: first, a clear understanding of yourself, your aptitudes, abilities, interests, ambitions, resources and limitations and their causes; second, a knowledge of the requirements and conditions of success, advantages and disadvantages, compensation, opportunities and prospects in different lines of work; third, true reasoning on the relationship of these two groups of facts. Since that time the knowledge and methods of vocational guidance have become a well respected discipline called career counseling.

Just as work is a vital part of our lives, so God is a vital part of career selection and development. Significantly, over the centuries theologians have developed a theology of work and calling that has deep roots in the Judeo-Christian scriptures. Many theologians have spoken to the issues of work, some with great power and length such as Luther and Calvin, and others with only a passing interest. Individuals and communities have been confronted by God's message that calls them to meaningful ministry, a vocation. Some responded directly like Moses. Others ran the opposite way like the prophet Jonah. Our career is impacted and shaped by our understanding of God's call. Vocation is our response to that call.

A survey of the current literature of career counseling finds it lacking in one vital area, a theological dimension. The disciplines of career counseling and a theology of work and vocation have not been integrated into the work of career counseling. One book, *Pastoral Counseling in Work Crises* by Henry H. Rightor (1979), and one unpublished Master's thesis by Thomas Brown entitled *The Presbyterian Minister as an Occupational Counselor*, are found at the Princeton Seminary Library (Princeton, 1962). There is within the church a cluster of twelve Career Counseling Centers under the Church Career Development Council that provides career counseling services for professional church workers. These career counselors are the practitioners of an integrated practice of career counseling and the theology of work, vocation and calling. This group has provided leadership in both the religious community and in the career counseling community. However, at this time, no formal material has been written spelling out the theory and practice of adult career counseling from a pastoral perspective.

It is out of this need that this book was conceived. The purpose of this book is to present a theoretical base for doing career counseling from a pastoral perspective as well as a step by step guide. Several issues such as career development and dual career families will be considered. This book will look at both theology and the assumptions of career counseling and then integrate them into a step by step journey of adult career counseling from a pastoral perspective.

This book is not designed to make pastors experts in the field of career counseling nor is it designed to make career counselors experts in theology. The purpose of this book is to present a practical integration of the two from this career counselor/theologian's per-

Introduction

spective. It is hoped that the uniqueness of this book will stimulate others in both fields to work closer together and explore further the interface. It is my desire to foster a climate of opinion that will encourage clergy and lay persons alike to recognize that work involves both God's calling and the person's clear self-understanding, aptitudes, abilities, interests, ambitions, resources and limitations. It is my intent to present a holistic approach to career counseling, one that expands the present models, methods and practice to include the spiritual dimension. Certainly, career counseling comes within the purview of the ministry of every Christian pastor/priest/layperson because Jesus called us to use our talents in God's service and thus experience life abundantly.

In an attempt to address these needs, this book will outline the basic assumptions underlying our understanding of work and the human potential (Chapter 1). Attention will be given to the theological understandings of calling, work and vocation with particular emphasis on the unique concept of vocation (Chapter 2). Career counseling involves a process of five steps. The reader is invited into a practical step by step guide to adult career counseling from a pastoral perspective (Chapters 3 and 4). Recognition of the developmental nature of career development and the issues present at each stage is examined (Chapter 5). One area calls for special attention, and that is the issues, drawbacks and strengths of the dual career family (Chapter 6).

Let me begin this journey with you by quoting from one of the most remarkable commentaries on career counseling. It is particularly remarkable because it was written in nineteenth century England.

> "Would you tell me, please, which way I ought to walk from here?"
> "That depends a good deal on where you want to get to," said the Cat.
> "I don't much care where," said Alice.
> "Then it doesn't matter which way you walk."
>
> Lewis Carroll, *Alice in Wonderland*

Career counseling from a pastoral perspective helps persons decide which way to walk. It is particularly focused on involving God as a partner in that walk.

Chapter 1

Our Human Resources

"What am I going to be when I grow up?" Each of us has considered this question at some time in life. I can recall one Saturday afternoon when I was in elementary school rushing home from the Saturday matinee with excitement and joy. Bursting into the kitchen I announced to my mother, "I know exactly what I am going to be when I grow up." Without missing a beat in what she was doing, she asked, "What is that?" "I'm going to be a cowboy just like my namesake, Roy Rogers." Up to that time I had hated my name, Roy. Now I had found someone to identify with and a job to go with it. Even then I knew I had to work. I just didn't know at what.

Throughout childhood we have vague hopes and aspirations of our life's work. Some of us dreamed of being a movie star, a firefighter, a pilot, an athlete or perhaps even president. School years are both fun and serious business. By the time we reach junior high, we become aware that our parents also have hopes and aspirations for us and often urge us to take certain courses in high school that will prepare us to get the right job. Often this is the work they expect us to do. Our parents have a powerful influence on our occupational choices, sometimes positively and sometimes negatively. Balancing their dreams with our dreams is not always an easy task.

For most of us our first exposure to work was a job that brought us money. Money seemed to make possible our dreams of the clothes we wanted, the car we really had to have, and the recording of our favorite group. We really didn't think that working in a fast-food restaurant was going to be our life's work but it did help get us the money we needed.

In high school by all likelihood, we spent some time with someone called a school guidance counselor who helped us to see what our potential might be, what openings might be available to us and what further training we might need. We then settled upon some course to follow, a dream, a hope to move toward. Sometimes this dream was simply to make enough money to keep us in those "necessities of life" we expected to have. For many, the choice of job was made even after college, based on the "first thing that came along" or a casual response to a want ad in the paper.

Stan, for example, works on an assembly line in a large auto plant. He has worked on this line for the last ten years, joining the company soon after graduation from college. He describes his job as repetitious and boring, and at times he feels as if he is on a treadmill. He is not sure that what he is doing is very meaningful other than it provides a small part of a larger automobile. He is finding that more and more joy in life comes not from work but from outside. He is asking the question, "If it's not satisfying, why do I stay?" In his mind he notes, "The money is good, the benefits are excellent." After spending four years in college preparing himself to be a math teacher, he had some difficulty securing a job. He followed the suggestion of his father and applied for a position at the same plant where his father worked. He had intentions of making this a temporary job, but after ten years he is locked in financially and is wondering if he will ever again pursue his dream of teaching.

Work: Joy or Treadmill?

Even with all our thought, preparation, and guidance this crucial decision of our choice of work seems to be based upon family expectations, social pressures, economic necessities, and sheer chance. John Oliver Nelson notes, ". . . rightly or mistakenly, millions of men and women work along year after year making the steady protest that this is not the right occupation for them, not the 'break' or the ideal work situation to bring out their abilities. . . . Much modern work is boring and deadening for anyone with creativeness or imagination. . . . Work nowadays tends to depersonalize people."[1] Workers are often isolated from the product they make, wondering what purpose or meaning their work has. We are increasingly becoming a service oriented society and moving away from a production oriented society. Even in our service orientation many people go to work, go through the motions, and collect a paycheck so they can do what they really find meaningful and enjoy—leisure.

Stan, like many people, spends a large amount of his time working and sadly works in a job he finds unsatisfying. In western society, work is a major source of status, identity and gratification. For the majority of people, however, work is an unsatisfactory experience that has become simply a job, a way of filling in time or earning money for the things that really are important. Almost eighty-five percent of the persons that come to the Northeast Career Center come because they are dissatisfied with the work in which they are engaged. They find that less than thirty percent of the work that they are doing brings any form of meaning, satisfaction or joy. Marsha Sinetar noted that ninety-five percent of the American working population do not enjoy the work they do.[2] This is a startling commentary on American society. Work takes more than one third of our time and is an integral part of our lives. If we are not experiencing meaning and satisfaction, then we are faced with a society in which workers may be going through a locked step motion, motivated more by money than anything else.

On the other hand, work has the potential to fill our needs and to bring joy and meaning, great satisfaction and even health. Work can fulfill the psychological needs to be confident and productive. It fulfills our need to function as a member of a team and a joint enterprise, to contribute to the welfare of the group and have some control over the means of our existence. Work, in fact, is a way of life. Adequate meaningful work also brings adequate and meaningful personal adjustments. These two go hand in hand. The kind of community, home, leisure activity, friends and joys in life go hand in hand with the nature of our work and the satisfaction that it brings. Work satisfaction and life satisfaction depend upon the extent to which we as individuals find adequate outlets for our abilities, interests, personality traits and religious values. Work may be that critical avenue of expression for each of us that does bring a deeper experience of meaning, joy, and purpose in life. Work is part of that intricate balance of life. If we experience joy and happiness in our work, then it provides the base upon which our whole life firmly rests. Like Stan, so many people put their dreams and hopes on hold and settle for a job. When dreams and hopes are put on hold, work becomes a treadmill. Those on treadmills feel trapped and yet know that life is more than this. People can get off the treadmill. To do so we need to take a look at what we are doing and why we are doing it. Ask yourself, "Does the work I do bring satisfaction, joy and meaning to me as a person?" "Is work an avenue through which I can express my full personhood and use my abilities and talents?"

Making Choices

"How do people arrive at the work they do?" What are the factors that affect and impact on people as they decide on and work at a meaningful, reasonable, satisfactory occupation. Stan followed in his father's footsteps but became bored and dissatisfied. It is a well established fact that each person has the potential for success, joy, satisfaction and meaning in a number of occupations. There is not simply one occupation that we can do but many. How do people get their ideas about what sort of work will bring happiness? How do some people get locked into a treadmill like Stan, doing work that is not satisfying, while other people find great joy, happiness, satisfaction and meaning in their occupation? Most people can find joy and satisfaction in a number of occupations. It is surprising why so many people don't.

This chapter will explore our human resources. It will look at those factors that impact upon us and the choices we make about our occupations. "How do we arrive at the work we do?" Making a satisfactory choice is not solely an intellectual task but rather one that integrates a complexity of factors involving the whole person and continual interaction with the environment. I will explore some basic assumptions that enter into the factors affecting and impacting on what work people do. These factors include the recognition that life is a dynamic process continually changing while at the same time predictable in life stages. We must look at the impact of our family of origin and its influence on who we are and what we do. Another factor considered is the realization that we are unique individuals and grow in our own special way. However, we must also note that we live within certain human limits and unique cultural influences that affect our individuality. We as persons are pushed by inner need. We are confronted at regular times by crises and thus the opportunity for change. It is important to note that each of us has occupational interests and abilities which affect our work choices and satisfactions. We all have a belief-meaning system that we need to be aware of. This is the vital spiritual side of the self that integrates our total life.

One of the most interesting stories in the Old Testament is the story of Jacob found in Genesis 25–33. Reading his life story gives us some very important insights into some of the basic assumptions underlying career choice and development. The story tells us of Jacob's long and difficult journey from "mama's boy" to the founder of the nation of Israel—a very unlikely candidate by human standards who through a series of events, personal and occupational stages and struggles, realizes his true vocation.

Developing a Career

Finding a meaningful and satisfying occupation is not something that happens instantaneously as Jacob found out. Rather it is a lifelong process of continual self-reflection, spiritual attunement, personal reflection and interaction within community and environment. The term "career" itself means a lifelong course of action or path traveled through life. It is a path traveled by each of us through which we can express our whole self and understand our vocation. The metaphor of the Scandinavian *parcours* is an excellent one for understanding a career plan. A *parcours* is an exercise trail with a set of planned stops where one exercises and develops different muscles or facets of the self. A career plan is like a *parcours* in that people can have several different occupations or stops as they travel along life's path, developing different talents and gifts at different times along the course.[3] As this metaphor suggests, career development is the slow, patient development of various talents, gifts, belief-meaning systems and self-insights over a lifetime.

The natural place for us to begin is to recognize that life itself is a dynamic process. It is a systematic series of actions, moving the person toward some end. At first, it appears to be so obvious. Life continually changes and is not static or stuck in one place. The movement that is the now quickly becomes past and we seem to be caught in an ever changing dynamic movement called the present. Since life itself is a dynamic process, so it is that our career growth and development is also a dynamic process over our life span. It is the continual interaction between the changing person and the changing environment. Thus change is always the constant. Each individual changes and grows. This growth is unique. It has no specific rules and can occur in many and varied ways, instantaneously at some point, slowly at others, depending upon the continual interaction between the person, the significant others around him or her and the environment in which he or she finds himself or herself.

Jacob gives us a good example of growth that is slow and cautious. He was born in a specific place to parents who had plans and expectations for him. He had a twin brother to relate to and to interact with. His mother guided his steps and encouraged and supported his ambitions of youth. He passed through the rite of passage into adulthood searching for his vocation. He worked for seven years to marry the woman he loved, only to be tricked and have to work seven more years, finally embracing his true vocation as his career path took him home. His growth seemed to take steps forward and steps backward with no instantaneous moment of major career change.

A contrasting biblical example can be found in Saul, who had an experience that turned his life around. According to Acts 9:3–9, he was on his way to destroy the Christian community when he was struck down by a blinding light and remained blind for three days. Through this instantaneous and dramatic experience, Saul became a fervent apostle for Christ and claimed his called occupation and pursued this career until his death. Career decisions are not static and career development is not fixed. Both Jacob and Saul show us that change is our constant companion on life's path.

Finding Your Own Pace

As we move dramatically through life we must move at our own pace and respect that pace as best for us. Integrating and assimilating experience, memories, events and the impact of people is the task. This continual slow internalizing and assessing of life's experiences is the way in which we begin to make sense out of the journey. Winston Churchill, for example, declared that his whole life had prepared him to be the prime minister of England at the outbreak of World War II. He had over his life integrated experiences and skills that prepared him to be the leader at such a critical time in world history. Clearly, there is not one process of development and aging but rather many. There is not one life course but many. There is not one set and rigid sequence of stages but many. The variety is as rich as the individual's ongoing interactions with persons and environment. Life is as varied as the individual's response at each turn, pause and obstacle. We can affirm with Krumboltz's theory of career counseling that life involves a dynamic interaction between persons and environment which means that change is constantly occurring or is at least able to occur. In other words, personality traits, interests and even self-concepts are capable of alteration at any point in life. The nature of the interaction between individuals and their environment is by no means simple but is highly individualistic and unique.

Moving Through Stages

As much as we would affirm the dynamic interaction between the person and the environment, there are in fact developmental stages and tasks which each individual must move through. This dynamic process involves the interaction of the person moving through these tasks and stages with the compromises and synthesis of the personal, spiritual, social and environmental interaction. Each individual, like Jacob, moves through what might be described as a series of stages, personally and occupationally, testing, questioning and affirming. The current work of the psychologist and the sociologist has given us a good understanding of the stages through which growth and development proceed. Obviously, these stages are not set, fixed or static, since life itself is a dynamic process unique to each individual. Thus the stages are simply guides describing the route.

In general, life can be divided into two very broad sections. The first part of life focuses on mastery. Here it is the task of the person to master many skills: personal, interpersonal and practical. In general the task is to develop the ego. For example, Carol, a twenty-five year old college graduate, was particularly interested in developing and mastering the business skills needed to move up the corporate ladder. She could discuss some issues of meaning but was focused almost exclusively on skill development. This is the predominant theme through the first thirty-five to forty-five years of life. The second half of life has, as its theme, meaning. Here the focus is on looking at the meaning and value of the tasks, consolidating learnings and social skills and asking the questions about what life is about. Peter at the age of fifty-three was concerned primarily with using his skills and mastered abilities in a meaningful way. "I want my work to contribute something, to meaning something in life," he noted. Those in the first half of life seem to be more oriented to mastery. Those in the later half of life are asking questions about meaning and spiritual issues. Naturally, both "task" and "meaning" are present in both early and later life, but one is dominant.

Erik Erikson reflects this emphasis on "task" and "meaning" in his helpful presentation of eight stages of development. The stages as he presents them are: trust versus mistrust, autonomy versus shame and doubt, initiative versus guilt, industry versus inferiority, identity versus identity defusion, intimacy versus isolation, generativity versus self-absorption, integrity versus disgust and despair. Without going into detail it is clear that individuals traveling along this road stop at each of these stages—sometimes for a short and sometimes for a long period of time. At each stop they deal with the issues at hand. The resolution and the satisfactory completion of each stage becomes the stepping stone for the next stage.[4]

Love, Anger, Sex and Work

Each person must deal with four basic issues in their developmental growth. These issues are all present before the age of ten and then in continual movement and flow are repeated a number of times throughout the balance of life. As these issues come to the surface again and again, it is an opportunity for growth, change and enhancement of the quality of our lives. The first issue is love. How do we receive love? How do we express love? This is the earliest experience of the child and is the basic developmental step upon which many of life's issues revolve. The second issue is anger. How do we receive anger? How do we express anger? Anger is a powerful force that can energize and drive us in many of our activities and relationships in life. Love and anger together are like the positive and negative poles of our life energy cell. Both are present, both are forceful, both are compelling and need expression. When either one is not expressed and not accepted as part of our core nature, then we begin to experience problems. The third issue that each of us meets is sex. Sexuality is a driving force in each of our lives, not only for procreation but also in our self-understanding, intimacy and pleasure. The fourth issue in personal development is work. As we grow we must learn what it means to be competent, skilled and contributing to our own welfare and the welfare of others. By work I mean the ability to provide for oneself through the use of mental or physical abilities or skills.

These four issues form the core issues of our developmental mastery and meaning. They are repeated over and over again at various times in our life. Bill, a forty-three year old man, reflected in counseling on his confusion about work direction and issues of love, anger and sexuality, stating, "What I'm doing is okay. No great earth shaker. At times I love it and at times I hate it all at the same time. The joy I feel is not so much in what I'm doing but in my talks with other people at work." He reflected later that he felt like a teenager again trying to solve the same problems as his sixteen year old son. These four issues come to us again and again especially at these transition times. The unique dynamic interaction of the individual would determine which of the four issues becomes prominent at which time throughout the process of life. We are not called to a static state in life but rather to a dynamic interactive journey.

Phases of Career Development

In occupational development we are invited in a certain direction, a career path. We travel as unique individuals through various stages of career development. Eli Ginzberg in 1951 introduced a developmental theory of occupational choice in which he presents three periods of development each with sub-divisions.[5] Up to the age of about eleven, he notes that children are in the fantasy period where their career interests are unrealistic and occur in fantasy. This is followed by the second period, called the tentative period, which is divided into four stages: interest, capacity, values and transition. This stage usually lasts from about age eleven until the age of seventeen. During this period young people define and clarify their interests, their work related skills, abilities and values they attach to work. They become aware of the necessity to make an occupational choice. The third period is called the realistic period with three stages: explorations, crystallization, and specification. During this period individuals narrow their choices while remaining ambivalent. They next select a career field, and finally they opt for a specific job or type of training leading to a particular career choice. This period typically concludes between late adolescence and young adulthood, although some people keep this option open much longer. It is helpful to see Ginzberg's theory as part of the early developmental career process of childhood and adolescence.

Donald E. Super focuses more on adult career development and presents what he calls a life span perspective which identifies the first transition from school to work. This transition is actually an adolescent rather than an adult transition. These are the years of exploration. The second transition he calls settling down. In the late to middle twenties sometimes early thirties, the period of unencumberment, drifting, floundering or trial comes to an end and the person settles down into the establishment of an occupation. This is followed by a third transition called adapting to stability and instability. This is the time in the thirties when the person seeks to adjust to a stable job. The tension here is the adaptation to stable occupation or instability. This is followed by the fourth transition called the maintenance stage. During this stage, a person has reached the peak of his/her capacities and his/her career. Super notes that people cope in one of three ways in this maintenance stage. First, they may stagnate either happily or unhappily. Second, they may update their skills and knowledge to keep pace with changing technologies and demands. Third, they may break out in new directions by innovating in their existing jobs or by changing to new fields or endeavors. This usually corresponds to the mid-life transition on a personal level. The fifth transition Super calls deceleration. This is the approach of the declining stage and is often accompanied by slowing the pace of work, reducing time and energy expended, dropping or delegating tasks to focus on others that are more congenial and lessening the commitment to work. This is followed by the sixth transition, adjustment to retirement. Super's transitional periods are helpful to note because of the concept of transitions. Transitions represent the continual movement and flow of the individual from one stage to another. The emphasis is on the positive opportunities presented at each turn as part of the ongoing process toward self-actualization.[6]

People make career choices not at a single isolated moment but out of the ongoing context of a lifetime of experiences. The past does influence current career strengths and difficulties and the future has its determination on present decisions. As a person moves through these transitions, it is clear that talents and abilities eventually surface as needed in the form of a burning desire and in response to the ongoing changes necessary in living. There is certainly good evidence that manifested aptitudes and functioning personalities are the result of the interaction of the person and the environment. The development of the individual through these transitions, personal and career, can be aided and guided by significant others, crises and opportunities presented to the individual as challenges. We must always keep open the opportunity for change and growth and new options as a result of the multifaceted interactions in our lives.

The Role of Family

In considering the question "How do people get their ideas about what sort of work they want to do?" it is natural that we look at the impact of family, parents, siblings, grandparents and other important persons in the early years of our lives. It is in the early years and the business of childhood that our adult personalities and work preferences take shape. Virginia Satir in her book *Peoplemaking* notes that the family is the most powerful social unit that forms who we are as adults.[7] Just as each individual is dynamically different, so is each family. In the family we learn to respond to crises, experience a sense of self-worth, learn to communicate, learn and understand rules and work through our need to individuate. Individuation is the lifelong process spoken about by Dr. Carl Jung. It identifies the force within us to claim who we are in relationship to others, primarily our family and parents. The roots of our career direction and occupational choices are clearly found throughout the early development of the individual and the impact that the family has on us.

This impact is vividly illustrated in the story of the birth and early life of Jacob found in Genesis 25. Scripture notes that Rebekah conceived twins and they struggled together within her. She inquired of the Lord concerning this and received the answer that two nations are in her womb and that one shall be stronger than the other and that the elder shall serve the younger.[8] Already before the birth of the children the mother had expectations and hopes for each of them. They will be leaders of nations and the younger will be favored by the mother. A second point is the realization that nature already is at work and we are given genetic differences, gender differences and biological differences that affect us the rest of our lives. Each person is born with a particular gender, a basic capacity and biological system for interacting with the world. Some persons are born with excellent physical equipment while others enter this world with handicaps and physical problems that dramatically affect their interaction with the world. This is in fact the given, the biological container with which we begin life. In addition we are born within a particular time of history, a specific culture and family system. These are the natural givens which cannot be changed. So it was with Jacob. He was born a twin. He was the second and thus younger son in a culture that gave everything to the first-born male child. Scripture records that at his birth his hand had taken hold of Esau's heel. Esau was his older brother by being born first.[9] We are struck by the importance of being a twin and the placement as second son in the family. This runs counter to the dreams, expectations and hopes that his mother, Rebekah has for Jacob.

The story goes on and gives us some insight into this family system by saying that when the boys grew up, Esau was a skillful hunter, a man of the field, while Jacob was a quiet man dwelling in tents. Isaac, the father, loved Esau because he ate of his game; but Rebekah loved Jacob.[10] Thus each child became the favorite and loved child of each parent. Jacob became mother's boy and Esau became father's son, each being taught and supported for their different natures which favored the parents. Thus we see that Esau, an extrovert, is encouraged and supported in his hunting and rough activities by his father, while Jacob, an introvert, is encouraged and supported by his mother to be a homebody and learn the ways of farming and domestic skills. Each son set on a different career path through birth order, parental support and personal character traits.

In the family we learn to understand our sense of self-worth. Self-worth is the feeling and value we attribute to ourselves through the messages and interactions with the family. Our self-worth can either be high or low given our experience with love, anger, sex and work in the family setting. These issues are modeled for us in the family. It is essential that people learn early that they are loved, trusted and capable. A large part of how we think about ourselves, how we view ourselves and claim ourselves as worthy comes from the way we think our parents saw us and treated us. Thus Esau and Jacob experienced love, but each from a different parent and thus in different ways. If the early messages tell us that we are loved, then we feel affirmed. If the messages tell us that we are not okay, then we feel negative about ourselves. Some families unfortunately give children both messages at the same time—you are loved and you are not okay. When this message is repeated again and again in the family, the child is left with a destructive and confusing picture of himself or herself. These family messages are carried by us into the future like baggage that can either weigh us down or assist us on our journey. Krumboltz points out that one of the important factors in career choice and development is the way we compare our performance, our skills and our sense of self to some standard drawn from the family. This is based on the way others treat us, particularly parents and siblings. It is from this that we draw conclusions about ourselves and our competence.[11] The family communicates to us feelings and ideas that we have about ourselves called self-worth. Do you feel good about yourself in your family? Did you feel good about yourself in your family as you grew up?

The second thing that we learn in the family is communication skills. Did anyone in your family listen to you when you spoke? In the family we learn to speak and to listen. We learn the skills necessary to let our feelings, dreams, hopes and wishes become known and expect some response. It is here we learn that verbal and non-verbal communication lets people know and not know us. In some families the communications are indirect, vague and not really honest. This form of communication creates problems. In healthy families where self-worth is high, communication is direct, clear, specific and honest.

The third thing that the family does for us is to help us understand the importance of rules. In the family, rules spoken and unspoken model for us the way we should feel, think and act. In some families, the rules are spoken with such force and directness that there is no flexibility for the individual to impact on the family rules. Thus a set of should and ought messages are provided that reside in our memory and impact upon our future. These become the expectations we have to live up to or down to. These messages tell us "You ought to be or do this" or "You should do . . ." The message may be about ourselves or about the occupation we "ought to" or "should" choose. Many people spend their entire lives doing what others think they "should" or "ought to" be or do. Much of this relates directly back to the verbal and non-verbal rules set down in early life. A second impact that the rules have upon us is that they become determining factors in the role we play in the family and in later life. Our role includes our biological place in the family as we identified in the Jacob story and the role our parents and siblings expect us to play. We may have the role of helper, baby star, pioneer or surplanter as Jacob did, or any number of other roles. The role that we are given and accept is played out in later life and may form a set of injunctions that determine how and what we do as adults.

This is seen vividly in the Jacob story when Jacob acts out the role and "ought messages" given to him by his mother. The story records that Jacob was boiling pottage and his brother came in from the field famished and asked Jacob for food. Jacob, the shrewd second son seeking to supplant his brother, bargains with him. He will give Esau something to eat in exchange for his birthright. Esau agreed. The birthright entitled Esau as the first-born son to the property and name of his father Isaac. Thus Jacob accomplished in this act of bargaining the fulfillment of the "should" message and role handed down to him through his mother. He was to be the special and favored son, the inheritor of the family name and wealth. Mother's dream and expectations had been integrated into the self-image of the son, Jacob.

The fourth gift that the family gives to us is the way we relate to other people and institutions outside the family. It is in the family that we begin to formulate our world view. We see the world either as a place to be feared, a place that is dangerous, a place to placate or to flame; or we see society and the world around us as open, hopeful, a place to dream, to work and to contribute.

Writing Your Own Script

Clearly these factors join together along with the environment and the society in which we are raised to set us upon a track that we tend to follow into adult life. The roles, the injunctions, our sense of self-worth and the rules all join together to give us a script, a subliminal program which becomes the parental or ancestral blueprint for our lives. A script is much like the blueprint that is used by the producer of a play. The script indicates the lines, the roles, the directions, the actions and the outcome of the drama. Each of us has a script. We are programmed consciously and subconsciously to follow the script. Our parents' behavior, choices and attitudes modeled for us and shaped our childhood perceptions, world view, beliefs and attitudes, views of realistic and unrealistic occupational choices. Each of us lives with countless inner directives. Each person's script is unique to him or her; that script can only be understood in light of that person's growth, development family, peer group, religious dictates, and a variety of other social sources that had impact on us as we grew up.

It is important for each of us to examine carefully our own script messages and the impact that the family has had upon us. Otherwise we may cling stubbornly to outmoded parental, peer or religious injunctions that limit, block or impinge upon our ability to be flexible, open and responsive to the many occupational options available in our world. In occupational choices, these messages come not only from the family, but also from the society itself. Being male or female has been seen for a long time as having certain occupational should and should not messages. For example, "Men should hold the positions of power. Jobs for men ought to be those demanding physical strength, management or money." "Women should be in service and nurturing occupations. As an extension of their mothering roles women should be nurses, teachers and secretaries." These have been the traditional women's work. It is very likely that these kinds of messages have been programmed into most of us. In reality, all occupations are legally open to both men and women. Yet many people still feel uncomfortable at the thought of performing certain jobs because they are men's or women's work.

Much has been made in literature of the importance of identification with parents and other significant adults in occupational choice and development. It is more complex than simply identification with a parent or significant adult. It is clear that childhood and adolescent identifications do play a significant role in shaping occupational interests. Stan, referred to earlier, was able to work in a factory after four years of college training for teaching because of his identification and admiration of his father. This is one other way that the family impacts on what we do and where we find satisfaction in our work.

Finding Yourself

The result of the ongoing dynamic development within the family and the community is the development of a self-concept, the ego. The early development of the child builds the self-image. This early ego is infantile, grasping, and seeking only security as a way of being. For example, as the story of Jacob's development continues, we read how Jacob at the encouragement and guidance of his mother met his ego-centered needs. The story records how Jacob with the direction of Rebekah tricked Esau out of the father's blessing.[12] This shrewd, tricky, ego-centered man joined forces with the expectations of his mother, thus stealing his brother's last gift from their father, his blessing. In this act the dream, hope and message begun before birth were fulfilled, and Jacob supplanted his brother Esau and became the stronger and first son in birthright and blessing. This young man is the prototype of the egocentric young adult seeking mastery, power, position and full blessing to satisfy his own ego needs, infantile and grasping. As time passes this ego-centered consciousness must surrender itself to the need to care, love and accept others. This is the beginning of a love that can give and serve others—agape. This letting go of the ego-centered self is a lifelong journey. After tricking his father and brother, Jacob flees and spends the rest of his life letting go of ego-centeredness and searching for a new balance between the needs of ego and the call of God.

When we let go of our ego-centeredness we experience a sense of self-esteem moving toward self-actualization. It is a commitedness, a mindfulness and a consciousness over meaningful choices. The letting go of the ego brings us into a new relationship with the meaning of life. This continued movement away from ego-centeredness is seen in six developmental issues. The first issue is identity, "Who am I?" The second issue is intimacy, "Can I be committed and close to another person?" A third issue is generativity, "Can I nurture myself and others?" The fourth is ego-integrity, "Am I satisfied with my life?" The fifth is trust, "Am I able to trust who I am, that I am committed and close to another, that I have ability to nurture and experience a sense of satisfaction with my life?" The sixth issue is meaningfulness, "Is my life contributing to a larger meaning of life?" These issues become the focal point as I grow and develop. I must let go of my egocentricity, which means letting go of the more infantile aspects of my own personality and embracing a more mature ego-self, a centered ego.

One of the stories about Jacob that illustrates this movement is found in the thirty-second chapter of Genesis. In the story Jacob meets a "man" who wrestles with him all night until daybreak, and in a show of magnificent courage in the struggle, Jacob holds his own and wins a blessing from his antagonist. The result of this was a change in Jacob's name from Jacob to Israel—a confirming through struggle of a new identity and a letting go of the egocentric self in favor of a new alignment of the ego and the self. Scripture indicates that Jacob was not simply wrestling with a shadow, a river demon, a devil, or even Esau, but with one who was able to bless him, change his name, God.

Several elements of the story stand out as important in our understanding of the development of self and occupation. Struggle involves a person at the core. The core of the person represents the very center; the human nature has polarity in drives and needs. I believe that both positive and negative exist in the core of each of us which are in conflict. This story of Jacob reflects the conflict. There seem to be two sides of human nature. One side is negative, and Jacob portrays this side through his manipulation, deception, theft of his brother's birthright and blessing. Jacob is all of these characteristics, and they are part of his very core. They are the unacceptable, limiting, frightening and frightened parts of ourselves. The other side of human nature is good and only needs to be brought out. Jacob's faithfulness is a promise to God, his constancy in prayer. His higher nature of faithfulness and love are present. This positive side of Jacob's core has a vision of angels descending and ascending a ladder from heaven to earth to minister to him. This vision speaks to the core of positive goodness in Jacob.

Taking Responsibility

What then is basic human nature? It is clear that both good and bad are present. The core of each person contains that which might be called the lowest and that which might be called the highest. The worst and the best exist together within us. Eric Fromm writes, "We must approach the unconscious not as if it was a god we must worship or a dragon we must slay, but in humility with a profound sense of humor in which we see that other part of ourselves as it is, neither with horror or awe. We discover in ourselves desires, fears, ideas, insights which have been excluded from our conscious organization and which we have seen in others but not in ourselves."[13] The willingness on the part of Jacob to struggle and his determination to secure a blessing from his struggles suggests that the goal of human development is to become aware of these polarities and accept their existence and seeming contradictions.

At best the person takes full responsibility for the polarities of these tensions. As a mature person, I must act responsibly and take responsibility for my own actions. Therefore, it is critical in self-understanding that I become aware of the hidden side of myself. It is part of our basic nature. When we try to ignore this part of ourselves it can become alienated as our dark side. We need to fully accept ourselves as we are. Until we can accept ourselves it is unlikely that our vocational uniqueness will reveal itself through us. Vocation is a way to live productively and uniquely. We learn to treat ourselves as if we count in our own eyes.[14] In the words of Sheldon Kopp, "It seems to me that the greatest problem belongs to those who turn away, who will not look unblinkingly into the darkness of their own hearts."[15] It is important for us to accept all of ourselves as we come to learn our limitations and strengths. This acceptance demands that we see ourselves as we really are. That which is in us that we fear is the very part that needs our acceptance and love, for we are whole people. The acceptance of the whole self and the process of individuation is a lifelong process reflecting itself in adult career development.

Fulfilling Your Needs

What we do with who we are is the key. There is within us a force that motivates us to become the person we want to be. The psychologist Abraham Maslow studied the relationship between needs and motivation for many years and suggested that it is what we need that motivates the way we act. He developed a hierarchy of needs which he diagrammed as a pyramid showing five levels of needs. The most basic level is called survival and is the base of the pyramid. At this level we strive for food, clothing and shelter. Our basic need is to stay alive. As this need is provided, a person is able to move to the second level, which is called safety needs. At this level people strive for more security, that is, savings, insurance, safe working places, safe home and a safe community. With these needs in place, the person is now able to move toward the third level which is belonging. At this level people work for good relationships with their family and friends, recreational opportunities and associations with groups in their community.

The fourth level is the level of self-esteem needs. At this level a person may strive for recognition and respect in his or her life's work and in the community at large. At work he or she may seek more autonomy, the right to schedule his or her own time and take more responsibility. It is at this level that people have the sense of feeling that they deserve to have a life, including a work life that makes them happy. There is a sense of self trust and they are able to solve problems creatively and assertively.

As these needs are met, the individual is pushed forward to the highest level, which is called self-actualization. At this level persons strive for the highest development of personal potential, including the establishment of individual goals and the ongoing growth of personal freedom, creativity, responsibility, mastery of skills, and accomplishment that is valued by the community, the family and friends. Occupation takes on a very special meaning and value. Sinetar notes that the self-actualizing person views work as a joyful experience, a calling that is more effortless for this person. Work becomes a way in which to understand life around him or her, a resolver of paradox and a path for personal development.[16] For this person work is a creative, graceful, personal and meaningful present moment experience. The push in each person is to move toward this self-actualization of the potentials which are within.

Clearly these various needs motivate each of us. Some people are able to move through the levels toward self-actualization. Others find themselves getting stuck at some level. Many people simply work to achieve the basic needs of level one and two. These needs must be fulfilled before the higher levels motivate the person. As a person begins to fill the needs at levels three and four, work takes on more importance and becomes helpful in developing a sense of confidence, mastery, achievement and creativity in one's life.

Finding Your Vocation

For many people their sense of self-esteem comes from their work. The fulfillment of the first four levels pushes the person to crave self-actualization. This deals with the concept of having a mission in life, a vocation. Work brings more than simply money or reward or that which is done simply to provide, but rather it now reaches the level of creative self-expression and often becomes the response of God's "call." Some of the characteristics that we have experienced with self-actualizing people is that work is playful and fun. It becomes an activity that permits the person to tune into the deeper, more truthful inner parts of the self. Work begins to be experienced as some of the best times in life and the person begins to function fully in each moment with energy and joy. The person is fully there, present, in what he or she is doing. Work thus becomes a fulfilling expression of the life force that is within each of us. Therefore the work becomes the fulfillment of the ministry and mission of that presence of God within. This work is called vocation.

Marsha Sinetar is helpful in her reflection of the traits found in common in the vocationally integrated, actualizing personality. She notes them as follows: "one, a sense of identity; two, the individual is able to and willing to consciously choose to do his work and to make conscious choices and take responsibility for them; three, his choices are prerequisite to his feelings that he has power, that he can create and that he has options, that he can make a difference, and that his actions matter; four, the individual is truly himself, more completely authentic and integrated as a personality and thus is able to bring the complex of his full, entire self to the work at hand. All his energies, talents, courage, attention and self are brought to work; five, work becomes a devotion, a labor of love, and indeed whatever the person himself might call it, a spiritual exercise, because the individual's concentrative powers, his choices, his actions and values are motivated, prompted and fueled by love. His service, as it were, is simply the enactment of his positive life force. His being or sensual self lies in all that he does."[17]

Building on Maslow's hierarchy of needs, Anne Roe points out that early parent and child relationships combine with other environmental experiences and the givens of intelligence, culture, gender and genetic influence to produce the needs.[18] A person's need of structure is greatly influenced by early childhood frustrations and satisfactions. Occupational choices are the result of personality which is in turn largely the product of early parent-child relationships. Career development depends on how the person learns to satisfy these basic needs. These needs are best satisfied by work through two predominant types of activities, those involving people and those excluding interaction with people. At the one end we have those persons who are interested in persons and at the other end those persons who are more interested in data and things. As we begin to reflect on occupational choice it is clear to see the impact that the family has on the person. The experience in the family combines with the social factors, self-concept and needs to produce interests in specific occupations.

One occupational theorist who is most helpful in understanding interests is John L. Holland.[19] He points out that if we know what a person is like, what his or her interests are, then we can predict what sort of occupation is most likely to produce satisfaction and achievement for that particular person. Conversely, if we can delineate a particular job clearly enough, we can assess what sort of person we should look for to fill that position. Based on interests on the one side and job descriptions on the other, he has put together six main categories. The first category he calls realistic; these are the body workers. These people enjoy working with their hands or doing heavy work requiring strength and endurance. Body workers work with objects such as machinery, plants or animals and like to be in the outdoors. The second major category is investigative. These are the persons who are interested in investigating and enjoy asking questions such as "why?" and "how?" in their work. They work with scientific or technical information, applying it to new situations. The third main category he calls artistic. These are the creative artists, people who express themselves through music, dance, drama, writing or art. The fourth category is social. These are the service people who find their rewards in helping people, such as teachers, nurses, and counselors. They often work in schools, hospitals or social agencies. The fifth category he calls enterprising. These are the persuaders, who like to work with people and enjoy convincing others to see their way. These persons often work in sales, politics, law and business where the success is measured by how well they influence others. The sixth category is called conventional. These are the persons who enjoy data and details. These persons use numbers or words in their work in a very exact way. They like to work without error and they often have good clerical or math abilities.

Every occupation fits into one or a combination of these categories. Each category attracts a different kind of worker and a different level of interest. Most people have a dominant category and one or two other categories of some but lesser importance. Holland makes a very convincing case for the fact that abilities and interests fall into patterns which distinguish one occupation from another and which distinguish one person from another. Holland points out, however, that personality traits and career interests may change over time. He points out that parents produce similar categories in their children both by modeling and by encouraging certain behaviors and preferences.[20]

Meeting Crises

It is a basic assumption that persons grow and develop in a specific way. They bring who they are and what they have learned into adulthood and are ever moving forward. The movement is toward maturity, health, wholeness or what Abraham Maslow calls self-actualization, and Carl Rodgers calls becoming. This movement toward maturity can be thought of as the process of God's creativity and saving act in the life of persons. It is clear that people are in such a process. This process is the process of becoming, of growth toward satisfaction and fulfillment. There is within us a natural force which pushes us in this direction. As a pilgrim moves along a road, so we move toward maturity and self-actualization. "Gradually my experience has forced me to conclude that the individual has within himself the capacity and the tendency, latent if not evident, to move forward to maturity."[21] This drive in us cannot be denied. We must grow or stagnate: physically, emotionally and spiritually. "Maturity is a road and not a fixed point or goal; it is a direction of movement and not a static point, a matter of degree and not an absolute state."[22] This pilgrimage toward maturity involves us daily in the issues of love and work as spoken of by Freud.

We are aware that this growth and movement in life is not always met with ease. Our path may be filled with tensions, strife, blocks and conflicts. We are met at each turn with challenges and crises. Life at times is unfair. We face a succession of emerging crises and problems as we go through life. Some of these problems are related to the various stages. Other problems are created by the baggage that we bring from our past, by the needs that push us and by the desire and dreams that we possess. Crises confront us.

The word crisis literally means a vitally important stage in the course of our lives which can become a turning point, a critical time or an occasion for change. In the Chinese language two characters form the word crisis. The one character means danger. The other character means opportunity. Thus the crisis is in fact a dangerous opportunity. How we meet these crises is critical to our satisfaction in both our personal and our occupational life. Satisfaction involves our willingness to believe in ourselves and our abilities, the resourcefulness that we have gained over the years and our determination to move on. When we are determined to meet life's challenges, we come to see that all crises and problems are opportunities for creativity, growth and new answers. In this way we tap into the resources that are within us, the resources we have developed that carry us through difficulties and help us move toward self-actualization. Career development is not a single relatively stable choice made once, but rather the culmination of results of present and past decisions, which are in fact subject to redecision. If our chosen career and options do not bring and provide satisfaction, we can change.

A critical skill that each of us must learn is the skill of decision making. There are three styles of decision making. These styles depend on the person's growth, development and learnings over the years. The first style is the rational decision maker who gathers information carefully, evaluates it objectively, and decides on the basis of likely consequences. The second decision making style is the intuitive decision maker who decides impulsively and emotionally according to current moods and thus allows little or no time to gather and logically appraise information or consider possible consequences. The third type is the dependent decision maker who takes no responsibility for decisions or for active involvement in the tasks required to make a decision and who is influenced by the demands and the expectations of others. These persons please passively. Research into decision making styles does not indicate that any one style is better or worse than any other style. The critical fact is that each must use his or her decision making style and skills regularly in moving toward a satisfactory career choice. The very best way to relate to an occupation is to choose that occupation rather than drifting through life. When we drift we cultivate self-doubt, passivity, poor judgment and apathy. When we take charge of our lives, then we choose to be responsible and develop self-esteem, creativity, assertiveness and a lively excitement and happiness in who we are and what we do.

Let me affirm the human resourcefulness, the dynamic developmental process through which all of us travel, the powerful impact that our families have upon our lives, the push and desire for individuation and the development of the self-concept that is congruent with both conscious and subconscious selves. I have affirmed the uniqueness of the individual amidst cultural and individual realities. I have affirmed the role that interests and needs play as both motivators and predictors and that there is within each of us the inner drive for self-actualization, growth and the natural corrective forces within. Each of us must take life in hand and through free choice and decision making direct our careers and our lives toward that enriching and satisfying career.

One additional factor must be addressed because of its powerful impact into who we are and what we do. We have a spiritual self that brings us into dialogue with God. This dialogue informs us about the meaning, value and nature of our life and work. Given who we are and what we bring to occupations, we must now ask the question: "What part does God have in my occupational choice and career development?"

Chapter 2

God and Vocation

Few people feel that their work is satisfying and meaningful. Millions who work in factories, corporations and services today see little connection between their work and God's calling. Few people ask the question, "What part does God have in my occupational life?" Instead of seeing work as our grateful response to God's calling, it becomes the means of gaining money, power, security, and mobility. There seems to be little incentive or desire to glorify God through daily work. We are all workers. We ought to enjoy our work and find meaning as co-creators in it. Certainly in modern industry and corporate life, it is work that has shaped our theology and faith, rather than our theology and faith shaping our understanding of work. With the growing pressures of economic security and needs, more and more time is spent working for money than working for meaning and joy. Is it then social pressures, family expectations, and sheer chance that determine the occupational course of our lives? Does God have a special work for us to do that will change our understanding of occupation and the way we earn a living? Does God in fact enter into our decision or is it purely human considerations? Many think that God is only concerned with those persons who are "called." "Call" in our day has come to mean professional religious service, ministry, priesthood, or religious life. Business, industry, and service occupations are often seen as "secular" and not related to or affected by God's call. So often people sense that God wants them to do something special with their lives and that they must leave the world and prepare for some special service in religious work. Such a narrowing of the understanding of God, persons and their work helps us identify the widening gap between work and God's call. We see an alienation of daily job life from God's presence, which has set off an anxious pursuit of material and physical substitutions for meaning, value, and the joy of glorifying God in our occupation. All our problems could be neatly solved if we could say, "No, God has nothing to do with my occupational decision." If you could somehow shoulder God out of the consideration, you could proceed with your preparation on your own terms only. But that cannot be done.

God's Call

God calls us to a ministry, a total life commitment. This calling touches deeply our understanding and involvement in work. To understand God's call and the place of work in our lives, the story of Adam and Eve in the book of Genesis is a good place to begin. It is a primitive archetypal story setting down the model for understanding this basic dynamic of God, persons and work.[1]

The Adam and Eve story tells us in very clear terms that there once was a time when man and woman were perfect. Their relationship to God, nature and the animal world was one of joy, caring, and harmony. A perfect relationship existed. They lived in a paradise, in a special, intimate and glorious relationship with God and creation. Adam and Eve were God's friends. They lived in intimate companionship, love and harmony, unmarred by distrust, injury, hatred, disharmony, competition, and envy. This story reminds us of the special wholeness that existed. The story thus sets down the archetypal model of health, wholeness and true balance between God, persons and nature. In this paradise amidst the intimate relationship and companionship, Adam and Eve were set to work. God placed them in the garden to till and keep it (Gen 2:15). Thus humankind was expected to work and to fulfill its part of a special covenant relationship in work. Adam and Eve worked in the garden. Nowhere in the story or in the Bible is there any indication that work is dishonorable, foolish or degrading. God expects us to work. Work in the garden also has a joyful connotation, which indicates that work is honorable, dignified, blessed and part of God's created order. It is part of the garden paradise. It can also be affirmed that God set the example for this work in the work of creation, calling Adam and Eve to be co-creators. Work belongs to us as God's stewards on earth.

The scripture writer wants us to know very dramatically in the Adam and Eve story that God created us to be at one with creation, to work as co-creators in harmony with God and nature. This paradise existed. Let us remember forever that there was a time when space, harmony and joyous relationships existed between persons, God, nature, and the animals. Work was a joyously shared meaningful activity. This is no idealistic dream but something that is a clear archetypal model carried deep within each of us. The symbol of this paradise is imprinted within our subconscious, pushing us ever forward seeking to reclaim this paradise again. It is important to note that in this paradise story, God and humans worked together. As Adam and Eve shared with God this co-creating occupation it became the unique vocation of Adam and Eve. Adam and Eve knew themselves and their relationship with God through what they did. This is the paradise archetype.

The picture then changes. Adam and Eve listened and were persuaded by the archenemy of God, Satan. Satan in the form of the serpent invited them to break the covenant relationship and claim a self-centered life. In this action by Adam and Eve the paradise archetype is split. God and the people are separated and their intimate relationship shattered. The choice was freely given and made to choose the needs of the self over the needs of the relationship with God. God demands that Adam and Eve must now leave the garden. The fall is thus symbolized in the choosing of self-centeredness over the balanced relationship between God and humankind. In the fall, Adam is told that he will continue his work, but now it will be made harder. Genesis 3:17 points out that because of their sin, the ground is cursed and thus the work of Adam and Eve will be accompanied by disappointments and heartaches. Thorns and thistles will spring up and bring frustrations and drudgery to work. Work then will become hard and a struggle. Work is not itself a curse, but the hardship connected with it is the curse, the consequence of the sin. The sin of Adam and Eve was egocentricity, seeking to become like God. Work is a curse when it seeks to be self-serving and meaningless. It then becomes an intolerable tedium which deadens the mind, the body and the spirit. It is the treadmill of life without meaning. Thus work for Adam and Eve after the fall is the arena for the potential for both blessing and curse depending upon its relationship to God.

The rest of scripture records the continuous efforts of God to mend the split and reestablish paradise. God continually reaches across the gulf seeking to bring renewed alignment. The efforts of God are culminated in the ministry and work of Jesus Christ as the new Adam, the God/man who restores the split in the archetype. This is Christ's work of redemption.

Meaningful Work

Work is thus a necessary and wholesome part of human life rather than a punishment. By work I am referring to exertion directed to produce or accomplish something. The word work has many connotations and is notoriously difficult to define. In scripture, work is used in three senses. First, it is God's work of creation and liberation. Second, it is Christ's work of redemption and reconciliation. Third, work is humankind's daily toil. The work of persons is part of our created nature.

> God created man in His own image, and God, the creator, was a worker. Man, in God's image, was therefore designed to be a worker. But, according to the Old Testament, sin entered. Man chose his own image of himself and attempted to negotiate life in that image. He saw himself no longer responsible to God but rather as being like God, with the knowledge of good and evil. The image just could not be carried off. It was not the truth about man, but a lie.[2]

It is then split in the archetype that brings about the sin. Work as seen in the Adam and Eve story is not a curse but is part of our co-creative relationship with God. God continues the work of sustaining creation through the work of Adam and Eve. This is continuing today.

When we define work as that done for pay, then we diminish the value of work itself and put the emphasis on the remuneration. As Dorothee Soelle points out, "When work means paid work . . . instead of viewing it as meaningful in itself, we relate work to compensation and value work according to its financial rewards. As we cleave to this ideology, we impoverish the meaning of work. We reduce it to a commodity, something devoid of meaning apart from the marketplace."[3] Meaningless work is a curse. Meaningful work is the co-creative relationship found in the Adam and Eve story before the fall. The symbol of Adam and Eve tilling and working in the garden is the image of God as creator and of all human work. After the fall, Adam and Eve worked for bread, struggling for survival forced upon them by the sin of choosing the image of self as split from the image of God. It is obvious that work can still be a curse in our time. It is a curse when it is meaningless and out of relationship and continuing conversation with God. Then it becomes an intolerable tedium, deadening the mind and embittering the spirit. It is a curse when it is done under compulsion for ends which the worker hates and against which the worker inwardly rebels. Work may still seem to many people at least in part a curse when it exhausts the energies and leaves the worker too tired to enjoy life.[4] This is the alienation experienced when work is separated from God's purpose, presence and relationship.

It is important to remember that God does reach across the gulf to seek to re-establish again the paradise and to seek a continuing conversation with us. This is a new alignment. This alignment is experienced in the letting go of the egocentric self in favor of intimate conversations with God. This change expresses itself in the arena of work as a major place of concern.

God's reaching out to us is the "call." God calls each of us and the community to a new and meaningful relationship and to loving service. The "call" of God is the action of God's love to us. It is God's love reconciling us, inviting us back into the harmonious relationship experience in the garden. Thus the call of God is always for salvation and service. In the Old Testament God's calling is the summons of God to the people of Israel. God summons them and thus claims them for service. Within this context of a national calling God calls certain individuals from the community for a particular task or occupation.[5] For the Christian, God's call is his invitation to accept salvation through Jesus Christ. In the New Testament we see God's call summoning the people to participate in the Christian fellowship, share the Christian hope, accept God's gift of salvation and a ministry of service. Again, from within this fellowship God calls forth some individuals to a special task of ministering to the called community, God's ministers and servants. God's call may come directly or indirectly, inviting us to fulfill some ministry, mission or function in his plan. "Calling" is from God alone and is always an invitation to the whole person to change his or her style and accept the good news of the gospel where the person is. The "call" relates us to the world and through the world. In this sense "calling" is a process and not a static event that happens once and is ended. We are continually being "called" by God to be ambassadors in the world. "A Christian call is not an elitist calling but an invitation to make something good and holy of our lives . . . it is a lifelong conversation with God through which we continue to hear hints and rumors of who we might become, of what we are to do."[6] Thus God's calling is not a mystical and abstract experience but God's continued reaching out to us through the many stages of life. God's calling relates to every aspect of life and affects our total life style. We need to remember that God works in history and in the world. God works in our history and in our changing world and calls each of us to reclaim now our paradise lost.

Vocation: Total Life Commitment

God's call demands a response. "Vocation" is our response to that call. Historically, the word "vocation" has meant "calling." It is the word used in scripture to mean God's call to the people. Vocation also has a second meaning implied in scripture: it can be used to mean the work which each of us does. In popular usage today the word has come to mean occupation, job, trade, or profession. In this book I will combine these definitions and use the word "vocation" to mean our unique response to God's calling in a "called occupation." Thus vocation is our response to God's call.

As God's call to us is the evidence of love and grace toward us, our response in "vocation" is our love responding to God's. In this act, we enter into intimate and ongoing conversation with God. "It takes a lifetime for God to show us who we are. Fidelity to a vocation is . . . the decision to remain in conversation with God."[7] Vocation is our commitment to a new and on-going conversation with God—one that continues throughout our lifetime. The fidelity of vocation is spoken of by Evelyn Whitehead: by our "continuing to communicate with God, to listen to God's voice in the successes and failures, delights and disasters of an adult life, we are more surely revealed to ourselves. Our vocations mature through the revelations and purifications of such a lifelong conversation."[8] Our vocational response is like the call itself, a lifelong process ever changing and responding as we change in our maturity, development and the understanding of both God and the world.

Vocation is a total life commitment and not simply an occupation. Thus our response to God's call can be the vocation of marriage, single life, or an occupation. The clear difference here is that a life lived as a vocation is one that is continually in dialogue with God responding throughout life to God's call for us to show love in our actions, to be servant and ambassador of the Gospel. "Vocation is a fundamental concept in the Christian life. . . . It is always a call to action. God, the creator, acts in the world and seeks our redemption. . . . Vocation is our life dedication and responsibility assumed."[9] Therefore, our response in vocation is our response in mission to find concrete ways of responding to the needs of persons, whatever those needs may be. By doing this and accepting the call we put aside our ego-centeredness and become preoccupied with our relationship in love with God and neighbor.

God "calls" and we respond through "vocation." On the one side we experience God's call and on the other side we see the necessity of work. There are many persons in the world who are involved in work and occupation only and earn a livelihood providing for the needs of self and family. Others are able to hear and understand God's call and move from an occupation to a "vocation."

God's Work in Our Lives
—The Story of Moses

The story of Moses found in the book of Exodus is another archetypal story which gives us some further help in understanding God's call and people's vocation. We are concerned here with the story and particularly with what it tells us about calling and vocation. It is the story itself that carries the message for our purposes and that informs us about vocation.

According to Exodus 1–2 Moses had a very unusual start in life. Born of Hebrew parents, raised by the daughter of Pharaoh, outraged by the Egyptian cruelty toward the Hebrews, he killed an Egyptian and fled into the wilderness to the land of Midian. In Midian he married and worked for his father-in-law, Jethro, tending the flocks. Thus after a stormy beginning Moses finds an occupation that suits him and settles down to work and raising a family. The rebellious adolescence and murderous act is forgotten as the young man settles into the tasks of young adult life, choosing an occupation and establishing a family. In some ways his choice of occupation, tending flocks, appears to be made by family expectations, social needs and sheer chance. However, God was at work in all of this to work for the liberation of the people. Moses is being schooled by his new family in the faith and history of his roots as a Hebrew. This is realized after the fact. We know the end of the story and so can look at God's work in the life of Moses. In our own lives we can also look back and see how events, teachings, family messages and what seemed at the time to be sheer chance happenings affected the movement from work and occupation to vocation that we are concerned about. How is it that some people find vocation and others spend their days simply working? Chapters 3 and 4 of Exodus tell us how this change took place in the life of Moses.

One day when Moses was doing his work, tending the flock, on the west side of the holy mountain, Mount Horeb, he saw a very unusual sight; a bush which was burning but not consumed. John Sanford in his book, *The Man Who Wrestled With God,* points out that "moved by curiosity, Moses approaches the fiery bush to see what this strange matter is all about. Giving in to his curiosity was the decisive step in Moses' life."[10] Curiosity is the motivating force in Moses at this time. We seem to be motivated by two very strong forces in our lives, desire and fear. These two instincts drive us to actions and reactions. We are all aware of actions taken by us that grow out of our fears. This is the heavy message of the "shoulds and oughts" in our lives. We "should" do this or we "ought" to do that. We are afraid and so we act. Desire is the other side. It is the push to fulfill our wants and needs. Curiosity is the desire to know or to learn something. Curiosity is not always seen as a positive force in our lives and can get us asking questions or seeking to know something that we later wish we didn't know. God can use our curiosity to involve us in a lifelong journey. "Curiosity, the desire to know, is a powerful instinct often used by God to draw us into life and our individuation."[11] Curiosity includes both our desires and our fears and draws us into growth opportunities and a search from which there is no escape. This instinct uniquely experienced by each of us is a powerful moving force inviting us from occupation into vocation. Moses was motivated by fear and desire, curiosity, to know more about this strange happening. This event will change Moses' life.

As Moses draws near he hears the voice of God calling from the fiery bush, and he responds, "Here am I" (Ex 3:4). It is this response that makes possible all that is to follow. This response opens up the lines of communication between God and Moses and begins a long discussion between them. This conversation lasts his whole life. Once we open up the lines of communication and respond in faith, then our lives are changed. Faith makes possible the response and the recognition that God has something to do with our day to day lives.

The response of Moses, "Here am I," reminds us of a similar story, the response to God made by the young boy Samuel, "Here am I, Lord." In this story found in I Samuel 3:1–18, God calls to Samuel, but Samuel thinks it is Eli, his teacher. Samuel gets up and goes to his teacher, but Eli tells him that he did not call him. Three times God calls to Samuel, and finally Eli instructs Samuel that the call must be from God and he should respond, "Speak, Lord, for thy servant hears." With this instruction, Samuel responds to God's call and hears the message of God. It is interesting to note that God does call and yet he is not always heard. Eli acts as a teacher and vocational counselor to Samuel. Then Samuel is able to hear and risks asking God what he is to do. For Moses it was his curiosity. For Samuel it was the counsel of Eli.

Each person recognizes God's call in his or her life through his or her own unique circumstances. For some it is at the right time and in the way that can be responded to by curiosity. For others it is at the right time and in a way that they need help in clarifying the call. God still speaks to us today and the "call" is present in today's world. "We do know that there is a type of inner experience which has this kind of numinosity and compelling power, and that there is such an experience as being called from within to a special mission in life."[12] Each person is called by God where he or she is and in a very different and unique way. The invitation to vocation, to do something special with our lives, does not usually descend upon us from external authorities, appearing predominantly as a "should" or duty. Rather, it is something from within us in our gifts, talents, abilities and best insights. Vocation takes root through the influence of loved ones, family, the witness of the community, caring mentors and guides, and a willingness to enter into conversation with God. Some people have an inner sense of God's call and know how to respond. Others only have clues, vague hunches and raw talents and need the help of a vocational counselor.

Returning now to the story of Moses, Moses has responded and recognized that God is calling him. Then God tells Moses what is needed of him. "I will send you to Pharaoh that you may bring my people out of Egypt" (Ex 3:12). Vocation is always a response to some action, mission or task. It is not simply taking on a role or recognizing that God called. It is a response that requires a life dedication to being part of God's plan for creation and liberation. For Moses it is God's call to be a messenger of liberation and salvation to the people. Discerning the action required of God's call in vocation requires further listening and conversation with God. It may take us a lifetime for God to show us our place as liberators and co-creators. It may mean taking a close look at who we are emotionally, intellectually, and in our abilities. The call of God draws us to use our whole self to follow in love, commitment and care for the world. It will require a change. To be in vocation requires not simply a recognition of God's presence in our lives but it must be fulfilled in action.

Once Moses hears God's instruction and call clarified into action, he has a very natural response—he argues and resists. He sees all the difficulties that will face him, and the curiosity of desire is now replaced by fear. He is not ready to give up the security and comfort of his present life and occupation to vocation. He is situated in a job with a wife and family to support. Why should he risk everything and follow God's summons. Besides, he is wanted in Egypt for murder. With this Moses begins to make excuses.

First, Moses wants to know that he will have a powerful, nameable authority behind him when he goes to Egypt. He is afraid that the people will ask who sent him and by what authority and he won't know. God tells Moses, "Say, I Am has sent you," and again Moses is instructed as to his mission. Again, Moses is afraid and says to God that the people will think he is crazy because he tells them that God sent him. And a second time God deals with Moses' fear and teaches him several very convincing miracles. Surely, this will overcome Moses' reluctance and he will let go of his fear and accept his vocation. Moses again tells God that he can't do the job because he is not eloquent and has a speech problem. God again deals with this fear, and by this time Moses has exhausted all of the excuses he can think of not to follow God's call. Moses then suggests that God send someone else. At this point God gets angry with Moses, assuring him that he is the one for the job. God will be with him.

Such are the efforts to get out of a vocation. It reminds us of Jonah who also heard God's call and, because it differed greatly from his own views and what he wanted, decided to leave. He demonstrates clearly the reluctance that we have to respond to God's call when it seems to go contrary to that which we believe or may even want to do. The call of God came very clearly to Jonah where he was and amidst what he was doing. Jonah, hearing God's call, fled in the opposite direction. God's call was asking Jonah to give up his hatred for Nineveh and his own self-centeredness. Not until he thinks he will die in the belly of the fish is he willing to relinquish his own self-centeredness of envy, pride, jealousy, and anger. He is able reluctantly to accept God's call and his vocation. His vocation like that of Moses is to fulfill God's purpose, not his own. Accepting God's call even when it is heard is not always done with great joy. It is often not easy to let go of our own interests and self-serving occupation and place our life in God's hand in vocation.

It is striking to see how reluctant Moses is to respond to the summons of God, how the dialogue begins and continues to resolution in vocation. The call of Moses does not suddenly re-educate him, give him additional talents and abilities. God's call to Moses does not suddenly make him better, wiser, or more sacred than any other person. Rather the call comes in the midst of where Moses is, who he is and with the abilities he has. The call is an invitation to a continuing lifelong conversation. God sees something in Moses and brings that forth from who he is now. The story does not stop here. Moses grows and changes through his lifetime. Moses, by his vocational response, becomes like a finely tuned string and resonates at the same vibration as the creator. Moses becomes attuned in his whole being to God. It is this attunement that is continually being refined, corrected, affirmed and experienced at each stage of development. Thus Moses responds to God throughout his life. God calls him again and again at various stages, and Moses responds differently at each stage. God's call does not occur once and then is over, but rather God continually calls us, meeting us at the various stages of our development and growth. As with Moses, God's call may be different at different times in our lives. When Moses accepted God's call and responded in vocation, it required an ongoing conversation, an attunement and a change in Moses' whole life-style.

The vocation of Moses is to liberate the people of God from their bondage. Moses invited the people to believe—to believe in faith and then act for liberation. This is God's call to the people through Moses. In order for the people of Israel to fulfill their vocation, they had to accept God's offer of liberation. They were called to trust God and accept their vocation as the chosen people who will be faithful to this vocation and a witness to the world. Moses does not call forth only some of the people but all of the people. They are called forth with all their various gifts, talents and abilities to service to God, to vocation. In this way, Israel collectively is called into a covenant relationship (Ex 20:1–20). In a special sense they are set upon a career path as the chosen people, traveling a specific path which will forever make them sensitive to God's continual call. As a nation, they too will change and grow through various stages of development. They must be in continued conversation with God both individually and as a nation. This is the national vocation of Israel.

The nation of Israel records the many times it strayed from its vocation. God in love sought it and called forth from the community prophets, teachers, and guides to help the people recognize again their special vocation. Jeremiah, Isaiah, Ezekiel, Joel, Amos, Micah, and many others, like vocational counselors, each in his own way, confront the people to be in vocation and fulfill God's call, individually and collectively. God singles out some persons for special work. Sometimes the calling seems perfectly matched to one's personal gifts, talents, background and preparation. Sometimes God seems to work through "unlikely" persons. At first the person called may not seem to have the talents needed for the job, but God often sees within him or her gifts and abilities that are below the surface and only become actualized through the growing conversation with God in vocation.

Discovering Our Hidden Talents—
Peter's Story

The story of Peter illustrates this point. In the gospel of John 1:42, we read that Andrew brought Simon to Jesus. "Jesus looked at him and said, 'So you are Simon the son of John? You shall be called Cephas' which means Peter.' " Jesus saw something in Simon that Simon did not see in himself. Jesus called him by a new name, Peter, which means rock. In this, the potential is identified and invited. Jesus saw the rocklike qualities that existed in this fisherman. God's call often identifies the potential within and invites it to be actualized. This is written about in a little different form in Luke's gospel story of the call of Simon. Simon, a fisherman, has fished all night and caught nothing. Jesus comes along and invites him to go out again. He gets into Simon's boat and they set out again. This time they catch so many fish that their nets were breaking. In this event, Simon was astonished and afraid at the same time. And Jesus said to Simon, "Do not be afraid; henceforth you will be catching men." And they left their nets and followed Jesus (Lk 5:11). It is striking to see the shift that occurs in occupational activities from fishing to fishing for men. The call takes a person where he or she is and redirects his or her life. The talents and abilities already present are refocused and given meaning and a place in the saving work of God for the people.

Simon was called where he was and in the work he was doing. He already had talents and abilities and was involved in an occupation. By responding to the call of God through Christ, his work became vocation and was turned completely around. The immediate response of Simon to the call was to feel astonished and afraid. Jesus had an image, a dream of what Simon could be and do. Simon caught a glimpse of the dream and was both astonished and afraid. Like Moses and the prophets called before him, God had to allay their fears and channel their astonishment. Simon was able to do this and through a leap of faith and trust accepted and responded to the image, the dream, the potential seen by Jesus. This leap of faith meant leaving something and claiming something. For Simon it was leaving the work in which he had been involved and the security of regular wages, home, community and family. It meant claiming a new dream, a new direction in his life that was part of the larger dream, God's dream for his life.

Christian vocation may be described as setting aside our fears and our ego-centered work and embracing God's dream. Simon saw the dream and followed Jesus. For most of us the image and dream of what God wants for us in this life comes slowly over a long period of ups and downs in life. "Vocational dream is gradually revealed to us in the various achievements and reversals of adult life. Since it is sometimes fragile, a personal vocation may be neglected and then wither, or it may become compulsive and too well defended."[13]

The response of Simon and his acceptance of his rock potential, Peter, was just the beginning. The gospel records the adult life development of Peter's vocation with its many ups and downs. The Acts reports this continuing story of Peter's growth and continuing response to the changing "call" of God in Christ. Sometimes Peter hears God's call in the interactions with people, especially the work of Paul. God's call is not a one-time act but a lifetime of dreaming, imaging, and responding. The image is one of ever widening circles as we move through adult life responding in continual conversation to God. Vocation always requires continuing nurture, clarifying, and purifying as we continually seek to know and understand what God is about in our lives.

The call of Simon to become Peter is instructive in that Jesus sees something in him that Peter doesn't see in himself. He had obvious weaknesses and they can be focused on. He also had potential. To see the potential in ourselves and others is to look and seek to draw forth what we can become. This is what God's call does. When we respond in vocation it is our willingness to accept the potential and seek to become a part of God's dream, co-creators in this life and culture. We are invited by the call to fulfill God's divine purpose to participate in fellowship, hope, and become instruments of God's love in action to others.

Putting Our Talents To Work

One of the striking parables of Jesus is that of the talents which tells us about people using their abilities or denying them. This parable, found in Matthew 25:14–30, tells us of a master who is going on a journey and calls all his servants together and entrusts to them his property—talents. In scripture the word talent meant an amount of money. However, the word talent today has come to mean the natural abilities of each person. Using this definition, the master gives to each of the servants abilities. To one he gave five, to another two, and to another one. Every person receives some talents, natural abilities. These abilities vary. Within each of us there are varieties of talents and abilities. God has assigned to everyone a life to lead and talents necessary to lead that life. It is a serious mistake to think that God has no interest in the daily work and the use of the talents.

In the parable, the master leaves each person to freely decide what he is going to do with his talents. Built into the story is the realization and knowledge that the master expects persons to use their talents. The choice is ours. The one who had the five talents used those talents and doubled his abilities. The one who had two talents also used those natural abilities and they increased by one hundred percent. The person who had one talent hid that talent. The master then returned to settle accounts and to ask what they did with the talents given. The question then of the parable comes sharply to the surface, "What are you doing with your natural abilities?" The expectation is clear: use your natural abilities in the service of the master. Each of us is therefore called to perform a task that is necessary for the on-going work of God's plan, salvation. Each has a responsibility to find his or her place and use his or her talents.

However, the point must be clear that we each have a choice. God's call to use our natural abilities in vocation is a choice. We can choose as the one-talent person did. God's call is the invitation to use our talents and our natural abilities in loving service, vocation. When this occurs, it is reaching beyond our potential into becoming and actualizing. The increase of talents in the parable by the five-talent person and the two-talent person is symbolic of the actualization occurring when we respond to God's call in vocation. Each person is a steward of the natural abilities. To use them in vocation means that they symbolically double. Not to use them in vocation is like the person who dug a hole and buried the talents.

Vocation is the symbol by which we respond to God and become co-workers, co-creators with both God and others. It is the continuing lifelong process of communication that helps us develop the natural abilities already present in the service of God and the community. Each has a choice for vocation in response to what he or she feels to be God's call. This choice depends on faith and trust. It depends on feelings that can be relied upon and a sense that this commitment and change is the proper choice for us where we are. It is accepting the natural abilities that have been entrusted to us and using them in the service of God. "Most of us are ill at ease when we are free. We would like for some outside force to show us clearly, unmistakably, and forcefully the direction in which we should go. But we are free and we cannot escape our freedom as much as we might like."[14]

The master gives each person talents and free will to choose. The parable goes on and each person is brought before the master to tell the master what he has done with his talents. The five-talent person and the two-talent person come forth and with joy tell the master how they doubled their talents. They are praised and rewarded. Then we realize that the parable is about the one-talent person who hid the natural abilities given because of fear. It is easy at times for us to identify with this one-talent person. Fears can immobilize, and we can sell our natural abilities short because we "only have one ability." We can easily beat on ourselves because we somehow feel less equipped than others. The one-talent person heard the master's call just as did the others. He chose not to respond. When this person is confronted by this, he not only identifies his fears but he blames God, noting that God is a hard master who is asking much in expecting us to double our talents and respond in vocation.

The ending of the parable seems unfair. The one-talent person loses even that talent. However, when we think about it, this is exactly what happens when we fail to use our natural abilities. We lose our abilities when we don't use them. When we don't use our talents, we in fact deprive others; we steal from them by withholding an idea, a word, help, or even our conversation. Responding to God by using our talents opens up potential, resources, conversation and ongoing dialogue with both God and persons. This is an on-going process, just as creation, salvation, and liberation are on-going. We, by accepting God's call, become co-creators, co-liberators, and instruments of God's salvation through vocation. The promise of God to us is very clear: "I've given you natural abilities. When you use them, then they will double. When you do not use them, then you will lose them." To respond to God's call in vocation opens up the dialogue to increase our talents and use them in willing service. Every person has a calling to manifest God's glory. The vocational response to this can be lived and fulfilled in many different ways. Every person is called by God to do something special with the natural abilities, to become someone special.

Called To Serve

Nowhere in the Bible is human work regarded as vocation in itself. God does not call people to be doctors, lawyers, or truck drivers. Such a notion secularizes the concept of call and vocation. Rather, God calls persons with talents, natural abilities, such as doctors, lawyers, truck drivers, etc., to be in vocation. Work, occupation becomes vocation when it welcomes God's purpose, to serve God and community in love. The calling is to service regardless of occupation. "Does this mean that God does not call persons to specific jobs? It means virtually that. The calling of God is a calling to salvation. It comes to you where you are. The priority, then, is not with the question as to what you should do but with the question as to whether you will admit God into what you are doing."[15] It is important to admit this and start here. God calls all persons to a lifelong conversation for salvation. Vocation is our total life response, given who we are and where we are. Vocation continues through all our life stages.

Regardless of how a person makes a living each one is to serve God. It is important to note that God's calling cannot be tied down to any particular activity. It extends to our total life commitments and life-style. It extends to all our hours whether on the job or not. It is difficult to distinguish working hours from non-working hours, since these are defined differently for each individual. We can clearly affirm that God's call extends to all of life, and thus our response is a total one. When we respond, then our motivation, involvement, purpose, meaning and reason for working are deeply changed and affected. This wholeness of meaning comes when we understand who we are as created in the image of God and are in continued conversation with God as co-creators. In vocation we recognize that we are both responsible and committed to God. "Without that meaning, the mature demands of our work will only expose the echoing emptiness in our life, or at best, stuff it momentarily with the unacoustical packing of sheer business. With that meaning, even the most irksome requirements of work can be transformed into an act of daily worship."[16]

The parable of the talents suggests that even though the master gives to each of us natural abilities, we are also given free will to decide how to use those talents. To use our talents in the loving response to God's plan for creation is to make occupation a vocation. Thomas Merton said, "Our vocation is not a supernatural lottery but the interaction of two freedoms, God's and ours."[17] Thus when choosing an occupation we lean toward using our God-given talents. We work to develop them and to increase the potential that is there. When we decide to put those gifts and talents at the disposal of God, then work becomes vocation. Again Michalson points out, "Work does not make us holy. Instead, we must make work holy. We must let our duty become our desire, not depending for meaning of our life upon our work, but letting the meaningful lives confer meaning upon our work."[18] In its true sense, then, work is in itself not vocation. Rather the work is one means of giving expression to vocation. Work must never become an end in itself but rather a means by which we can show God's love and serve God and neighbor. Every person is called by God to do something with his or her life and to be something for God. This is the message of Ephesians 4:1: "Lead a life worthy of the vocation to which you have been called."

Called To Be Co-Creators

What does it mean to be called? Simply this—we have accepted the summons of God in the good news of the gospel. The first creation is unfinished. Creation continues and is an on-going process. Thus we accept our place as co-creators called to a continuing conversation with God and to announce God's love to the world. To be in vocation then means to put aside love of self, selfishness, and become preoccupied with love of God and neighbor. Work is the arena of action where we demonstrate our letting go of selfishness and embracing a new relationship between ourselves and God, the ego and the self. This creative relationship is "holiness." The word "holy" applies to both God and humanity. "The traditional concept of holiness pertains to our co-creative role with God in alleviating human suffering and making justice in the world."[19] All are called to this mission. It was the whole of Israel that God called. It is the whole Christian community that God calls. It is the whole of humanity that God calls to a new heaven and a new earth, the paradise lost. Thus our vocation is to love God and to love our neighbor. God's call to Israel and the fulfillment of that call in Jesus Christ is the sending of his followers into the world to witness to the truth they had seen in Christ and our seeking to be faithful now through the Spirit at work among us. Thus all persons are called. There exists only one kind of calling by God and that is the call to discipleship. Occupation is a vehicle for this calling.

From this called community some persons are singled out for the purpose of teaching, instructing, healing, and leading the community. In both the Old Testament and the New Testament, individuals were set apart as ministers to the ministering community. These persons served as God's vocational counselors, persons called from amidst the community to challenge, teach, and witness to God's continuing call and our continuing need to respond in vocation. It is clear that first a person is called to community and then some may sense a call to be "ministers, priests, religious." They are given the responsibility to minister to the called community. H. Richard Niebuhr points out that all persons are called to the discipleship of Jesus Christ, to hearing and doing the word of God, to repentance and faith. Others experience a secret call, namely that inner persuasion or experience whereby a person feels himself or herself directly summoned or invited by God to take up the work of the ordained ministry.[20] It is important to note that this secret call, as Niebuhr identifies it, is limited to those who would be servants and ministers within the community. It is the believing community that recognizes and verifies this call in a person and trains him or her to be their leader.

Not all persons are called to be "ministers, priests, rabbis, religious." However, I think that many people experience both a general call to serve God and a personal calling to use their abilities and talents in ministry. The uniqueness of this personal call is the shift from occupation to vocation. The fact is that most of us have many talents and abilities and could do a number of jobs well. The choice is up to us. This choice becomes vocation when we are willing to open continual communication with God about our life's direction and God's needs. To be open to God's call and at the same time aware of the talents and abilities we have makes possible vocation. This requires commitment. Many options might be available to us. Choosing and exercising our freedom in conversation with God eliminates many anxieties about vocation. The point is that each of us may decide. The "call" of God is the invitation to choose that occupation that will be most serviceable to our on-going sense of God's will. It is in this way that our personal call may direct us into a unique vocation. It is clear that vocational change may not require an occupational change but rather a reorientation of our sense of purpose and mission within our present occupation.

It is important to note briefly that there is no reference in the New Testament to the idea that one vocation is higher than another. God calls all persons through Jesus Christ to use their abilities and talents in a vocation. One vocation is not higher than any other, and we must hold firmly to the idea that there is no separation between sacred and secular vocations. Christian vocation is sometimes equated with full-time Christian service. This is not the case. To be in vocation is to respond to God's call in our on-going work—doctor, lawyer, truck driver, clergy. Much debate has occurred in the history of Christianity over this issue from the rise of doctrinal disputes, the granting of special status to clergy by Emperor Constantine, the development of monastic orders, the impact of the crusades, and the reformation work of Luther and Calvin. It is important to affirm that the biblical view of calling is that every person is summoned to salvation service and on-going conversation with God without distinction between clergy and laity. God can be, and is, glorified in the workaday world when we respond to God's call in vocation. Vocation is the means of implementing God's call through loving service to God and to the neighbor in work. People can serve God in work whether it is a menial job, a profession, or a business. We need to remember that vocation embraces the totality of a person's life. "A quiet revolution is occurring in the land. Ancient distinctions between clergy and laity are giving way. A time-honored separation between Christians who 'have vocations' and those who do not is being bridged."[21] This hopeful change will lead us to bridging the gap that has existed and still exists between occupation and God's calling. It is clear that we are in that current vocational crisis—the crisis of the separation of God's calling and occupation. It is the absence of a sense of vocation. The Chinese character for "crisis" is made up of two separate characters meaning danger and opportunity. The crisis we are in is in fact a dangerous opportunity. It is a time to be hopeful.

God's purpose has been, is and will continue to be the re-establishment of the paradise lost. God continues to pursue humankind in call. We are all born with abilities and talents. Throughout the stages of our lives we may become aware of these talents. We may develop them and choose to use the talents in various occupations. Work is not God's punishment. Rather, it is our opportunity to share God's call for liberation, the establishment of peace, justice, and a renewed on-going conversational relationship. When we despair that the separation that occurred at the fall seems to have become increasingly wider, we need to remember God's ever present and persistent reaching across the gulf. Creation continues, liberation continues, salvation continues, and we are continuingly being called to vocation at each stage of our lives. Vocation takes a lifetime, and we are called over that lifetime. God calls us as we are with the abilities and potentials we have at each turn of our journey. When we respond to God's call, our occupation takes on the qualities of vocation. Through vocation we experience a new and on-going relationship with God that changes our direction, brings meaning, purpose, and an invitation to self-actualization to our lives. Vocation is the connection between the secular and sacred through the journey of a lifetime.

Discerning God's Call

Over the centuries all religious groups have sought to identify ways to connect the sacred and the secular. How do we know the will of God? What are the ways we can know God's will for our occupational lives? Before beginning on your career decision-making process, in the next two chapters I will identify some of the ways that you can use to better know and understand God's call. Naturally, discerning God's will is an on-going process, not a single event used at the time of crisis. The disciplines of the faith bring us into the presence of God weekly, yearly, over our lifetime. Just as we must take the time to practice our talents such as music, art, writing, speaking, so we must take the time daily to practice our spiritual disciplines.

Traditionally the spiritual disciplines of prayer, Bible reading and study, worship and group sharing practiced regularly bring us into the environment that makes possible attunement with God. It is expected that these disciplines are a regular part of our lives as we seek to choose our vocation. What I am talking about is the need for us to be in committed continual relationship with God. Relationship with God is renewed every day, and must be seen in the on-going process of where I am and where the divine is. I know God in relationship and experience God's salvation, acceptance, love and anger, guidance and wisdom for vocation through our meeting. The relationship is primary. No person can be a Christian alone. The spiritual disciplines invite me into a changing relationship with God, others and myself. Martin Buber develops these concepts in what he calls the "I-Thou relationship." Worth, personhood and direction are experienced in the I-Thou relationship, God affirming me as a person in our relationship and I affirming God. This is where God's Spirit is at work. Martin Buber defines the Spirit, "The spirit is not the I, but between the I and the Thou. It is not like the blood that circulates in you but like the air you breathe. Man lives in the spirit if he is able to respond with his Thou. He is able to, if he enters into relationship with his whole being."[22] The relationship is that which is between us.

That is where I meet God, in the I and Thou that exists between myself and the other, and in the I and the Thou that exists in myself. In my relationships I meet God and I know that I am loved, trusted, accepted and challenged to a vocation. As I listen and relate I discover both the internal needs and the external needs that open my mind, heart and soul to vocational response. When I relate only to the world in an I-It relationship, then it becomes impossible for me to see God at work in the world. Claude for example walked down the same city street for years. One morning after returning from a weekend retreat sponsored by his church in which he was renewed again by the spiritual disciplines of faith (prayer, worship, Bible study and conversation) he saw a "street person" standing in a doorway along the street he had walked down for years. The regular practice of the spiritual disciplines opens us up to God's message for us through persons.

In my relationship with others, I need to care and listen to where they are. By listening to their words, their feelings, I find the relationship strengthened and renewed which brings God in as a vital part of life. It is here that I experience being heard and being in tune with God, the depth of being. When I am able to do this and to really listen, then I experience a joy of renewal of my vital energies, my connectedness to God and direction for my vocational life. This I experience in meditation, prayer, worship and most vitally when I relate authentically to others. Through this on-going authentic relationship I enter into a continual dialogue with God. Out of such a relationship comes that presentation of vocational opportunities and the awareness of how I can respond to God's call.

One unique way that we can be aware of God's call in our lives is through our dreams. As John Sanford pointed out, dreams are God's forgotten language.[23] The scriptures are rich with stories of God's direct communication through dreams, visions and the visitation of angels (a special form of the dream). Dreams are a form of direct communication that connects us to God. God speaks through the medium of dreams and visions not in direct words but rather in symbolic images, sounds, and colors. Dreams then are a vital tool in spirituality, a way of listening and communicating with God and the inner spiritual world. Dreams are a valued part of discerning God's call and our response in vocation. Dreams give us clues to the vital inner life of each of us, spiritually and emotionally. Some people give very little attention to their inner life and hence may not remember dreams. Others learn to pay attention to this rich resource. These

God and Vocation

persons use their dream life to help them understand who they are and where they are going.

Dreams give us many clues to our life situation, including information about our fears, anxieties, relationships, tasks, unfinished tasks, and vocational direction. Not all dreams will direct you vocationally but all dreams will help you live a fuller, more satisfying life when they are appreciated and understood. Dreams are like political cartoons that need to be read and interpreted. Remember, the dream has a message for you about yourself, your strengths, blocks, fears, joys and direction. The first step, of course, is to remember your dreams and write them down. A dream is like a letter that needs to be opened and read. One method for understanding and appreciating the meaning of your dream is to sit in a chair with an empty chair opposite. Imagine your dream or a part of the dream to be occupying the empty chair and ask the dream what it has come to tell you. Then switch chairs, pretend you are the dream or a part of the dream, and start talking. You may be surprised at what you hear. In this way you will be able to use the dream to help you find the creative solution, to understand God's message for you and about you. Continue your conversation with the dream or the parts of the dream until you are able to come to some understanding and a positive outcome from the dream. You might try asking yourself, "What would this picture-story mean if it were a cartoon of my life at this moment?" Dreams are another vital spiritual discipline that you may choose to use in discerning God's call and your response in vocation.

I invite you now to take all of you through a career decision and development journey. Bring all of you, mind, spirit, emotions, talents, abilities, interests and values through an adventure seeking your vocation.

Chapter 3

Getting Started

Agnes, a black woman, grew up in a culture aware of her race and gender. She claimed her uniqueness, her abilities, gifts and talents, and sought to use them in the service of God. She sensed clearly that God had a ministry, a special vocation, for her and had summoned her to be the unique self-actualizing person she could be through vocation. Vocation for her is her response to the inner sense of God's call. She has some ideas and clues as to what this vocation might be, but it ranges from teaching, social work, and music to hospital administration and ministry. She is seeking to join her talents with her sense of calling but is not sure how.

Through vocation we can join together the sacred and the secular. How do we go about doing this? Is there a clear way to arrive at a vocation? Persons make such a decision by choice rather than by chance. Choice means inviting change. For change to take place, we must be willing to be sensitive to who we are, where we are, what we want and what God wants of us.

The setting for change is part of the on-going life experience of each of us. We are confronted at each turn by opportunities and invited to change in many ways. We seek to move from dissatisfaction to satisfaction, from meaninglessness to meaning in our occupation. We are the only ones who can say to ourselves, "I will change," and then do it. It is easy for us to see where others need to change and how they may be wasting their lives in a particular job. It is more difficult for us to take a look at ourselves. It requires us to be curious. It requires us to be motivated. It requires us to act. It requires us to be anxious about the potential and opportunities available. It requires us to be engaged in on-going conversation with God which will keep us ever questioning, ever searching, ever reaching and ever growing. When we conclude that we are not engaged in the occupation that is fulfilling, enriching and self-actualizing, then this is the time for us to reach out for help. When we are able to recognize our needs for help and change, then we have solved fifty percent of our problem. Career counselors are those persons especially trained to assist us in career choice and career development. Some career counselors are additionally trained to assist persons in discerning God's call and our vocational response.

I have decided to use the term "career counselor" for several reasons. First, the term career is a contemporary term that is increasingly supplanting the word guidance. It is used to designate and encompass the developmental nature of decision making as a lifelong process. The term career development is that term used to mean a lifelong process of getting ready to choose, choosing and continuing to choose from among the many occupations available in our society. Second, the term career includes the concept of vocation. The career counseling process is that process used to assist persons in identifying, claiming and developing the on-going conversation of vocation. To help in the interpretation of God's call is the responsibility of the career counselor who is pastorally oriented. Third, the term counseling has been selected rather than guidance to refer to a specific interpersonal process focusing upon assisting a person or couple to make appropriate career decisions. In career counseling there is more room for information than in psychotherapy or insight counseling, although the same principles apply in both. Advice has little place in career counseling. Guidance on the other hand often has the connotation of a "test them and tell them" program of job orientation. Counseling involves a relationship between counselor and client that does not consist simply of giving tests and reporting the results, but is a process that often embraces personal, marital, and family issues. Career counseling goes beyond this to explore and explicate the client's role in one of the main areas of life, the world of work and our vocation in it. Career counseling not only facilitates career development (choice and adjustment), but it also enhances personal growth and spiritual development. Fourth, the career counselor who seeks to counsel from a pastoral perspective integrates into the counseling process the questions that are related to the relationship of God and persons. Such questions are: "What are the ways we discern God's call?" "How can we bring our occupational life into continuous conversation with God?" "Are we willing to enter into vocation?" Career counseling is a clearly defined process. Like any other specific branch of knowledge it has methodologies, a system of principles, practices and procedures. It takes into account both personal and career issues without allowing the structure of any model to take precedence over the needs of the person. Career counseling is a holistic approach involving self-understanding of the total person, mind, body, spirit, emotions and environmental impact. It is a very specific tool available to us in helping us meet our vocational crises and assists us in arriving at a meaningful, reasonable and enriching vocation.

When you go to a career counselor you should expect the counselor to tell you who he or she is, what his or her approach is and what he or she charges. You should expect him or her to tell you what his or her understanding is of the relationship between occupation and God's call. It should be the first task of any career counselor to give you adequate information for making an informed choice about whether or not to proceed with the counseling. It is particularly important for the career counselor to reassure you about the confidentiality of the process and the limits of that confidentiality. Career counselors who are not willing to tell you their educational training and the types of persons and problems they are best qualified to deal with should be avoided. This is usually given to you at the first visit or over the telephone. It is important for you as a consumer of career counseling to be an informed consumer. In purchasing any product or service, ask questions about that service and be sure that it fits your needs. When it does, commit yourself to it.

Career counseling follows a five-step process. As you proceed through this material I would invite you to be a participant in this process. Travel through a *parcours,* an exercise trail, stopping at various places to do one or more exercises which will develop different muscles or facets of you. I would invite you in this career *parcours* to take some time to stop and do the various exercises presented and to reflect on your own vocational commitment and direction, your self-understanding and career development. By choosing to work through this systematic journey, you have made an important decision to reflect on your present and future career plan and vocational affirmation.

The exercises in this and the next chapter are *not* intended to be a substitute for career counseling but rather are appropriate for anyone seeking to explore and clarify his or her vocation. The process will be useful for those seeking to understand themselves, explore their work world, discern their vocational direction and move toward launching their vocation. The vocational direction for each person is only good for that person if it has a growth potential, utilizes the person's talents, reflects God's calling and enriches the self and others. It is important to reaffirm the uniqueness of you in relationship to God's call in your life.

Career counseling moves through the following five steps which present a unique opportunity to engage in a systematic search for vocation. First, time is spent assessing needs, identifying dreams and goals, and making a commitment to change. Second is the step of data gathering. It is an opportunity to take a close look at yourself and to begin to understand who you uniquely are in your interests, abilities, relationships and selfhood. Another phase of the data gathering step is to look at career options and to explore the world of work. This phase involves developing and refining career alternatives. The third step is that crucial step of choosing your vocation. Fourth is the step of launching your vocation. It is the step of making a plan which will move you toward your targeted vocation. The fifth and final step is that of the vocational search itself. It is the specific marketing of the self to gain the right vocation. Obviously, the process is completed when you secure your vocation and begin to use the whole self in it.

Step One: Assessing Your Needs

The first step in moving toward a vocation is to assess your needs. What do you want to accomplish in this career counseling process? This is the time to set goals, visualize your self-actualizing vocation and claim those areas in your life and occupational world that need change.

It is helpful in beginning this process to secure a large notebook. Use this notebook to record regularly your thoughts and ideas as you go through the journey outlined in these chapters. The value of writing in a notebook is that it helps document the journey. It slows you down and helps you become a better observer of yourself. It will help you record in a systematic way the progression of the exercises to follow. In this way you will have a specific opportunity to become more aware of the many subtle and bold ways that your inner and outer worlds impact on you. Your notebook becomes a journal to record your progress along the career *parcours.* There will be times when you will be asked to set the book aside and focus on a specific exercise. By doing this you will maximize the reading of this and the next chapter. You are invited to make entries into your notebook and record your thoughts and insights. Sometimes you may be experiencing a persistent dream, symbol, image or thought that should be recorded for further reflection. Remember that your goal is to discern God's call, identify your resources and move to a response in vocation. As you become involved in this process many of the events, ideas and reflections that happen to you at this time may have an important bearing on gaining insight and tapping into your rich inner life.

God may speak in the small voice of symbols, dreams, persistent images, ideas, insights and prayer. God speaks to persons directly through inner reflection, prayer and dreams. Scripture presents in great detail the many times God has chosen to speak to a person through these means. This direct communication with God continues today. Therefore, throughout this journey it will be increasingly important to pay attention to your inner life, your prayer life, and especially your dreams. It is your way of being sensitive to God's presence speaking to you through the symbolic language. Record these images, visions, dreams and prayers. These are some of the very specific ways to discern the will of God and remain in lifelong conversation with God. This dialogue moves our occupational explorations toward vocation. Be open to the possibility and the need for some change in your life and in your work. Approach the whole process with the expectation that something significant is going to happen. A change is possible. Commit yourself to do what is necessary to make that change happen to you. You are at the beginning of an adventure that will enable you to take charge of your life and align yourself with God's will through a vocational choice.

The place to begin is to envision a personal and vocational future that will bring you happiness, one that will use all of your gifts and talents and draw forth your vital abilities, your personal energy and the realities of who you are in relationship to others, God and yourself. Your future begins in the present with the dream of who you want to be and what you want to do. The best clue to the vocation that will bring you meaning and fulfillment is as close as your imagination. Take some time now to close your eyes, breathe deeply and rhythmically, and relax. In this relaxed place imagine your future vocation. Imagine that you can do anything you want to do. Set aside any blocks or limitations and let your imagination take you to that dream vocation. Picture yourself engaged in the vocation in as great detail as possible. What are you doing? Where are you working? Do you work alone or with others? Be as specific as possible and set aside the limitations as you consciously think about them, i.e. gender, culture, time. Spend fifteen to twenty minutes in this relaxed and quiet place envisioning your actualized vocation. Before going on, take the time to do this exercise now.

When you are finished write a description or draw a picture in your notebook of your visioned vocation. Be as specific as possible. Take the time to read what you have written and let your conscious mind take in this dream without judgment, questions or negative comments at this time. This is your visioned vocation.

Given this visioned vocation, expand your thinking to include other parts of your life such as marriage, family, recreation, geography, income, etc. In the many areas of your life what is your preferred future? A preferred future is owning the future that you personally and vocationally prefer. It is just as easy to live your preferred life as it is to live a life of chance. To help you focus on your preferred future write at the top of the next page in your notebook the statement, "BEFORE I DIE I WANT TO . . ." Complete that statement in as many ways as possible. Be as specific as you can. Take the time needed to do that now.

Certainly, many of the items that you have listed and that you want to do in your lifetime may have nothing to do with your vocation or the world of work. However, some of them will and probably could be considered part of your visioned vocation. Look over the items again and think about each item on the list and compare those items with your visioned vocational description. Circle those items on the preferred future list that could be accomplished through your visioned vocation.

You are now ready to write down your goals. Given your preferred future and the reflections on your visioned vocation, write down as specifically and as concretely as possible your goals for this career search. What do you want to accomplish? How can you use the systematic steps of this career process to clarify and accomplish your goals? Take the time now to write this in your notebook. Write at the top of a new page, "MY GOALS ARE . . ." As with any journey it is difficult to know when you have arrived at your destination if you do not know what your destination is.

With these three items now in place—your visioned vocation, your preferred future, and your list of specific goals—you should have a clear idea of what you need. You will be able to answer the question, "What is happening now in my personal and occupational life that makes this career process a helpful journey?"

Step Two: Gathering Data

The data gathering step of career counseling involves two parts. The first is a close look at yourself. This self-assessment seeks to help you understand who you are. It focuses on family, needs, abilities, talents and spiritual clarification. The second is specific help in refining career options.

Self-Exploration and Understanding

The purpose of this step is to explore and understand the self as a unique person. You are full of dreams, hopes, expectations and history that can promote and resist your claiming vocation. You are both what you have been and what you want to be. The goal of this part of the process is to look at what you have been and understand who you are.

Family Legacy

Our family legacy is those experiences, messages, biological and emotional strengths and problems handed down to us by our family. We have been affected, changed and directed by who we are, where we were born, and the family with which we grew up. Too many people do not follow their dreams and preferred future because of how they view their past. It is, therefore, important for you to look at your past and reflect on the strengths and blocks handed down to you through your family legacy.

Take some time now to reflect on your family story. This will help put into perspective the many aspects of you. This exercise is aimed at giving you an overview of your history, your story. Draw your lifeline. A lifeline traces the major events and experiences in your life such as: birth, early childhood events, illnesses, school, peer relationships, moves, marriage, children, your religious experiences, your work life and significant events. You may wish to reflect on whether these times were ups or downs for you. What were you feeling at particular times? Use crayons or colored markers to express the feelings present in the event. Take a large sheet of paper and express your story from birth to now through colors, ups and downs, circles, drawings, words and/or lines. Take the time to do this now.

Upon completion reflect on where you have been in your life and how events, persons, and situations are now informing your visioned vocation.

There is much that can be learned from looking at your history.

Some things will become very obvious at first glance. Other things will need some reflection. What is obvious about your history? It is natural to remember events that impacted on your life and to forget others. Peter drew his lifeline, and as he reflected on his drawing he noticed that he had not put down his father's death. He was in college at the time and was torn between finishing school and going to work. He felt responsible as the oldest son to take care of the family and go to work. He is still working for the same construction company fourteen years later. It is helpful to share your lifeline with a spouse or friend. Ask them what they notice. What stands out as obvious? Others are often perceptive and sensitive to patterns and events that we may overlook.

It is often helpful to reflect on the colors that you used. If you used colors note the predominant color. This will give you a general feeling and tone for your life. Colors mean different things to different people. What do they mean to you? In general, there are three warm colors: red, orange and yellow. There are three cool colors: blue, purple and indigo. One color stands in the middle between the warm and cool colors as a color of harmony, balance and growth, and that color is green. The warm colors are in varying degrees of passion, anger, love, sexuality and spirituality. The cool colors are the colors of detachment, coolness, reserve and distance. Persons who predominantly use reds, oranges and yellows are expressing their passions for life. This includes both anger and love. Persons who predominantly use blues, purples and indigos are expressing their reflective nature, their thinking, analytical approach and reserve with emotions. Blacks and browns are usually earth colors. Black is sometimes used as a pen reflecting little thought to colors. Sometimes black mixed in with other colors along your lifeline might symbolize a sense of grounding or may note times of earthy reflection. What are the colors in your lifeline telling you about you? Consider the impact that this has or may have had on your career choice and development. How does it relate to your visioned vocation?

Look at the content of your lifeline. Were there repeated patterns? It may surprise you to see that over your life's journey ups and downs come in a rhythm, perhaps by year, perhaps by events, perhaps by repeated stress. Life for most of us is not simply a straight line but a series of circles moving us ever forward. For example, Carl became aware that he followed a pattern of getting a new job or going to a new situation, then having a difficult first year. This was followed by several years of outstanding success leading to several years of boredom. At this point he discovered that he moved on to a new job or situation, to repeat the pattern again. As you reflect on the ups and downs of your lifeline do they reflect for you a sense of failure and success? What precipitated the down patterns of failure? What helped you turn these around and move up to successful living? Linda realized that her down times related to her need to be a super woman. She was working very hard to be all things to all people: super wife, super mother, super social worker, super daughter and super student. This repeatedly brought her to a place of burnout which was followed by a time of exhaustion. At this point she reclaimed her own needs and wants and began to take care of herself. When she set aside time to do what she wanted and gave herself some care, then she was able to let go of being super-responsible for everyone else. At these times she felt alive and growing again. She saw in her lifeline this pattern repeat itself three times. Many events and pressures in life can knock us down. Life at times is unfair and painful. All of us know that we do have resources that can help us stand up again. For some these resources are family, friends, faith, claiming the creative side or owning anger and converting it to creative self-assertiveness. What helps you stand up and move forward again toward self actualization? Does your lifeline help you identify when you used your resources? One of the most important resources available to us is a clear direction in career. Moving on from the now with a clear visioned vocation can help break some of the negative patterns.

A second exercise that is helpful in reflecting on your family legacy is to identify the predominant role you played in your family. Each of us is given a role or takes on a role which is the part we play or are assigned within the family system. Take some time to reflect on your role. In your notebook write at the top of the page, "ROLES I PLAYED IN MY FAMILY." Then list those roles. You may want to check with other members of your family and ask them what role or roles they saw you playing in the family. Do this now.

Some of the roles found in families are:

1. The Harmonizer. This is the person in the family who keeps peace, who negotiates different points of view and helps when there are disagreements and arguments between persons. This is the mediator who works for compromise and harmony in the family.

2. The Rebel. This is the person who is considered the black sheep, the one who always does the opposite of what is consciously asked in the family. He or she may be in fact drawing off negative feelings in the family like a lightning rod. This person takes the

negatives of the family and acts them out by jest, sarcasm or actions. In this way he or she diverts unpleasantness in the family and draws it to himself or herself.

3. The Pioneer. This is the person who explores new thoughts, behaviors, values and reaches out beyond the family system into new areas. This person is often the first child. He or she wants to know what is over the next horizon.

4. The Watcher. This is the person who follows, who goes along with the family, somewhat passively accepting the ideas of the family. He or she serves as an audience at times during family discussions, actions and activities. He or she is the listener in the family.

5. The Encourager. This person is friendly, warm, responsive to other members of the family. He or she praises others. This person helps others express their best self by agreeing with and accepting the contributions that others are making in the family.

6. The Responsible One. This is the person in the family who takes responsibility upon himself or herself for the family. He or she often feels responsible if something happens to a brother, sister, parent. This person takes upon himself or herself an unnecessary amount of weight, usually for the family's happiness. These are just a few of the roles that can occur in a family. Describe your role as unique and special to you. Identify your place in your family.

Since the family is the primary group in which we learned our roles, these roles may become so ingrained in us that we cannot change them. One role may be more dominant than another. Sometimes we have more than one role in the family. These roles carry over into our occupation selection and development. They may be a large determining factor in the type of occupation we find attractive to us. The occupation will be congruent with the role that we played in our family. Cindy, for example, was drawn by her inner intuition into family therapy as her career choice. As she explored her own family history and the role she played in the family, it became very clear to her that she was the harmonizer. She kept the peace and negotiated differences between her siblings and her parents. At times she remembers trying to mediate tensions between her mother and father. Her career choice of family therapist was an extension of her already established and practiced role in her family. The more we know about the roles we played, the more we can choose to continue or change them. Knowing your role will greatly assist your career reflection and development.

A third exercise that is helpful in reflecting on your family legacy is to be aware of how your family has influenced you by giving you expectations. These are called "should messages." A should message is a message spoken or unspoken that tells you what you should or should not be or do. All of us are given these expectations. For example, Jill was given a clear message, "You should go to college and you should get married." Living up to these becomes a driving force for her as she dates men, looking at each one as a marriage partner. Others get messages like: "Don't get married." "You should serve your country." "You ought to be a professional." "Be a doctor." "Women should . . ." "Men should . . ." These should messages have such a powerful impact on us that we may spend our lives personally and occupationally doing what others think we should do, not what we want. When we get caught up in doing what others think we should or should not be or do, we experience the tyranny of shoulds. These messages are given to us by authorities in our past such as parents, teachers, religious leaders, counselors, peers and those persons we decide are authorities for us. Should and ought messages if unexplored or unexamined may rule our lives and drive us into situations that do not meet our needs. We may be in an occupation because of these messages and be missing the joy and fulfillment of vocation.

Take a moment to think about the should and ought messages you live with. Write them down in your notebook. Take some time to do this now.

Now take a look at these should and ought messages. Ask yourself which ones really matter and which ones need to be set aside. How important are they? Who gave them to you? Many of your should and ought messages form your religious belief meaning system and are very important to you. They help you experience fullness in both your personal and your occupational life. This happens when your belief meaning system is congruent with who you are and the values to which you commit yourself. Others may need to be changed, in that they feel tyrannical, controlling and limiting to your full relationship with God and neighbor. God calls you and you are invited to respond in vocation. God's call is not a heavy should or ought message but an invitation to be the best person you can be in relationship to him. God invites you to use all your talents, abilities and gifts in an on-going movement toward self-actualization.

These exercises and reflections hopefully have helped you see the powerful impact that families and authorities have on each of us. They inform you about which occupations are acceptable and which ones are unacceptable in adult life. They open the way for vocation.

Other messages, roles and history that you have brought into your adult life may or may not help you move toward your visioned vocation.

Need Reflection

Abraham Maslow has given us a good understanding of the five levels of need that motivate us.[1] In the first chapter the work of Maslow was noted. Maslow identified the levels of needs as: (1) survival, (2) safety, (3) belonging, (4) esteem, (5) self-actualization. In beginning to understand yourself and what motivates you it is important to reflect on the levels of needs and how they motivate. List each need on one side of a page in your notebook and record your thoughts and feelings about each need next to it. Do that now. Then ask yourself the question, "What level of need motivates me the most?"

Since each level is a motivator, each level must be dealt with, beginning with the first. When we have met the needs of the first level, then we can move on to the next. If you have decided that you are motivated by level five, self-actualization, remember that the first four levels of need have to be largely fulfilled. Naturally, we all move back and forth up and down the need levels at different times in our lives. In some areas, we may be dealing with social needs, while at other times we may need to go back and spend time on safety needs. All of us crave self-actualization but few of us claim it. It is on this fifth level that we reflect about God's call and the concept of having a mission in life and not simply a job. It assumes that work and occupation are more than simply meeting the first and second needs, survival and safety. Take a look again at your motivating needs and ask yourself the question, "What am I doing to fulfill my need for (1) survival, (2) safety, (3) belonging, (4) self-esteem, and (5) self-actualization?" Record your answers in your notebook.

It is clear that you are not starting from zero. There are a number of things that you are already doing to fulfill your needs. Every person is doing something in a unique way in some or all of the needs levels. Look now at your list again and add to that list those things that you could do to fulfill your needs in each level. The emphasis is on "could do."

Having identified the motivating need factors, relate them back to your visioned vocation. Reflect on how these needs are motivating and informing you to fulfillment of your visioned vocation.

Identifying Your Abilities and Talents

Let us now look at your native abilities and talents. What are the strengths unique to you? Every person has his or her own uniquely strong abilities and talents, but some people fail to see them or claim them. These need to be identified before you can move on to exploring your vocation. Clearly it won't do much good to worry about what someone else might claim as abilities. You can only claim and use your own. A good vocational choice is partly based upon identifying, claiming and using your strong natural abilities. Affirm the God-given talents and recognize that you have unique talents and abilities that are part of your inner richness and resources.

In your notebook list as many specific accomplishments and achievements as you can remember over the last ten years. An accomplishment and achievement is some event, activity or goal satisfactorily completed. These may be large or small, work-related or events in your personal life. They are the areas in your life in which you have satisfactorily completed something whether it was formally recognized or not—for example, "I made a dress." "I graduated from college." "I learned to use a computer." "I made a bookcase." "I taught someone to read." Write down as many accomplishments and achievements as you can think of in your notebook.

Now go back over your list and select the top ten achievements and accomplishments.

On the graph (Figure #1) list these top ten accomplishments and abilities across the top. In the left hand column you will see a list of abilities. For each accomplishment and achievement mark an "X" next to each ability you used while completing each achievement and accomplishment. Take the time to do this now.

Now total up the number of "X"s for each ability used and place that number at the end of each bar. Total the scores for each section and record them in your notebook as a score for DATA, PEOPLE, THINGS, and IDEAS. What is your reaction to these totals? Do you have more abilities in one section than in others? Consider all the abilities for which there is a score above "0" and divide that list into three equal columns: Highest, Middle and Lowest. For example, if fifteen abilities are scored, you should have five in each column. Place the three column headings in your notebook and list the abilities under them. Do this now.

You are now ready to describe yourself based on your identified major abilities. Write in your notebook a self-description using your

Getting Started 65

Figure #1

	I: ACTIVITIES					II: ACHIEVEMENTS					
ABILITIES	1.	2.	3.	4.	5.	1.	2.	3.	4.	5.	

PEOPLE

	1	2	3	4	5	1	2	3	4	5	Score
1. Mentoring/Counseling											
2. Negotiating											
3. Instructing/Teaching											
4. Supervising/Managing											
5. Persuading/Influencing											
6. Speaking/Performing											
7. Serving											
8. Listening											

Total scores for PEOPLE

DATA

	1	2	3	4	5	1	2	3	4	5	Score
1. Synthesizing											
2. Coordinating											
3. Analyzing											
4. Computing											
5. Copying											
6. Comparing											
7. Researching											
8. Observing											

Total scores for DATA

IDEAS

	1	2	3	4	5	1	2	3	4	5	Score
1. Organizing											
2. Innovating											
3. Developing											
4. Expressing Written Ideas											
5. Reading/Studying											
6. Mental Picturing/Visual											
7. Clarifying											
8. Memorizing											

Total scores for IDEAS

THINGS

	1	2	3	4	5	1	2	3	4	5	Score
1. Building											
2. Designing											
3. Financing											
4. Purchasing											
5. Operating											
6. Inspecting											
7. Repairing											
8. Collecting											

Total scores for THINGS

abilities list. For example, "I have abilities in . . ." Now list your abilities.[2]

Good vocational choice builds upon native abilities. When we lead with these native abilities, then we have a firm base upon which to build. The parable of the talents gives us additional insight as previously noted, so that when we use our talents and abilities, then they increase. How do your native abilities and talents help you affirm the reality of your visioned vocation?

Spiritual Clarification

God is a vital presence in all our lives. For some people this is very obvious. Other people find it hard to sense God's presence at all in their lives. Look back at your lifeline and reflect on God's presence in the various events and coincidental happenings. Perhaps there were identifiable and persistent times when God was present guiding you or seeking to touch your life. Ask yourself the question, "Where have I felt or experienced God's presence in my life?" Life seen from this perspective is a continually on-going conversation with God toward the visioned vocation. As you look back at your lifeline, are there identifiable and persistent patterns that seem to emerge?

This is an appropriate time for you to reflect on your faith. Listed are a number of questions which I have found helpful in exploring and clarifying my faith. Take some time to answer the questions in your notebook.

List three words that describe your faith.
Describe one belief about which you are very certain.
Describe one belief about which you have considerable doubt.
Describe an action you took because of your religious faith.
How does your faith affect your occupational choice and development?

After reflecting on these questions, the answers led Bill, for example, to a very important decision. Bill realized that he had natural abilities in the areas of managing, persuading, influencing and research. This led him to consider a number of occupations. One of these occupations required him to work in the weapons industry. He thought about this in great detail and asked himself if this was what God was calling him to do. The money was very good and he would be able to provide for his family and enjoy some of the things he wanted. After reflecting on his faith and his religious values, he concluded that God was not calling him into this field and that it was incongruent with his faith to work in a weapons industry. Upon further investigation he found another company where he could work. In this second company he realized that this was reflecting his values of peace, justice, harmony and love. He felt called to this place and responded through a commitment in vocation.

When our religious-belief-meaning system is not congruent with our work we often experience the continuing stress, frustration and dissatisfaction in both our spiritual lives and our occupational lives. When we are able to move toward our visioned vocation in response to God's call, then there will be congruence between what we believe and what we do. Do not be afraid to be faithful.

Self-Understanding Through Tests

As part of the self-understanding step of career counseling, counselors often use a number of testing instruments. Among these might be included the Minnesota Multiphasic Personality Inventory, the Sixteen Personality Factors or the Myers-Briggs Type Indicator. These tests are a valuable tool; however, it must be emphasized very strongly that tests are just that—a tool. Few counselors would accept the mechanical use of tests. Taking a test and examining the results is not magical. No test can identify the person's uniqueness. No tests can tell us what is in the heart and soul of a person. Tests do have a valuable place but only in the context of the counseling process. Test results need to be interpreted and understood by a professional in light of the person taking the tests.

I personally, in career counseling, have found the Myers-Briggs Type Indicator to be very helpful in providing preference feedback for personal understanding. It can give the person some productive insights as to his or her dominant way of relating to people, taking in information, solving problems and sorting out data. The test is one of the most widely used instruments in career counseling. The results usually give the person some helpful clues as to what occupations would be congruent with his or her preferred personality type.

Naturally, the more we know about ourselves and understand both our past and dreams for the future, the better able we will be to move along a track toward our visioned vocation. Self-understanding is a continuous life process as we move through the various developmental stages. We can take advantage of its opportunities for change and for growth. We can build upon our best selves to become the person God wants us to become in our total life, personally and vocationally.

Career Options

The second part of the data gathering step of career counseling is to develop and refine career alternatives. This is done by building upon your best understanding of yourself. Having looked at yourself, you are now ready to shift and look at the world of occupations. This is a complicated step because it involves more reflection, integration and considerable back-tracking. It needs you to both reflect on your past experience and be open to the unfamiliar possibilities. Looking for new and different career options means setting aside your old frame of reference and risking something new. This can create anxiety and tension. People tend to move back to the familiar when anxiety and tension increase. It is similar to a thermostat that is set at seventy degrees. When the temperature moves below or above seventy degrees, then the thermostat activates heat or cooling to bring the temperature up or down to the seventy degree setting again. So it is with each person. When we have our mental expectation thermostat set at a certain level we tend to operate and think at that level. If we think of being less or better than our set expectation, then we experience anxiety. We move our actions up or down to bring us back in line with our set self-image. To consider the unfamiliar is to change our self-image which risks anxiety and tension because it may differ from our set self-expectation. Change is exploring new possibilities and is always accompanied by tension. Change is exploring and accepting the unfamiliar career choice. Be open to the unfamiliar.

This step is also complicated by the fact that there are a tremendous number of career options. It is impossible to know about every job and every occupation. Thus we are immediately confronted with the overwhelming nature of a vast amount of occupational information. We certainly would want to have complete access to the latest information and a clear understanding of the latest career trends. Unfortunately, rapid changes in the world of work and in the economy, coupled with increasing efficiency and complexities of occupations and with new occupations arising each day, make it impossible to know about all occupations. However, information is available, and it will become necessary to systematically explore it based on your self-understanding, abilities, interests, and inner sense of God's call.

The first aspect in developing and/or refining your career alternatives is to go back to your lifeline and identify more specifically your work history. Where did your work? What did you do? Now, identify the jobs that you did and list them. Next to the jobs, list the tasks involved in each job. Take the time now to list each job in one column and next to it describe the tasks involved in doing that job.

Next to each task write what you liked about the task and then in the next column what you didn't like about the task. (See Figure #2)

For each task you may wish to ask yourself, "What skills did I need for the task? What new skills did I learn for the task? How well did I perform the various tasks? What one or two changes might have made the job either more or less enjoyable?" It is helpful to reflect on the impact that your values had on you. Ask the questions, "How did the job affect my life outside of work? Did I feel it was moving me toward a greater sense of satisfaction and self-actualization?"

Your past work history may have been more by chance then by choice. However, by examining and exploring the tasks involved in the jobs you did, you will begin to get some clues as to what was satisfying and what was unsatisfying. Take this information and again begin to relate it back to your visioned vocation.

Let's look now at your career interests. Careers cluster into six basic groups. These basic groups attract people with similar interests. People with similar interests are drawn to each other and are usually drawn to the same types of occupations.

Try this exercise: Suppose you are at a large picnic where the people are grouped according to their interests and occupations. Imagine yourself mingling with each group for a short period of time.

Group one are the body workers. These people enjoy working with their hands or doing heavy work requiring strength and endurance. Their interests include physical activities, body work, working with objects, practical machinery, plants or animals, and they like the outdoors.

Group two is the investigators. These persons enjoy investigating, researching and searching, using questions like why and how. They are interested in what makes events or practical things happen the way they happen. They are interested in computers, medicine, science and research in general.

Group three is the creative artists. These persons are artistic people who express themselves through music, art, dance, writing, and creative expression through the media. They have interests in plays, books, and art in general.

Group four is the service workers. These persons are involved in helping others through service such as nursing, counseling and

Figure #2

JOBS	TASKS	I LIKED	I DISLIKED

teaching. They are interested in people and are concerned about serving others.

Group five is the persuaders. These persons like to work with other people and enjoy persuading, convincing and influencing them to see things their way. They enjoy sales, politics, and law and would be interested in selling to people.

Group six is the data detail people. These persons enjoy math and using numbers and words, and they want to do things in a very precise and exact way.

Having mingled, to which group do you instinctively find yourself drawn? Which group is second? Which group is third? Identify these three groups as one, two and three and record them in your notebook.

Now go back and relate them to your visioned vocation. Would the persons and occupations that to you were drawn to belong to your visioned vocation group? Is the group to which your visioned vocation belongs the same group as the one you selected at the gathering? If so, this is a strong indicator that your greatest work satisfaction may be found in a vocation in that group. Usually, people are drawn to more than one group and find that combinations of two or three groups are their best career choices.

Several tests have been developed that use interests to help you be more precise and thorough in selecting one or two of the six groups. Career counselors may use the Strong Vocational Interest Blank or the Strong Campbell II. These tests are helpful, reliable and available to most people through college placement services. They may be on a self-directed computer system. You may wish to check at your neighborhood community college or nearest college to see if it has the self-directed vocational interest inventories. If so, take it. You can then sit down at a computer and answer the questions and begin to work through the above process in a more detailed way.

The third aspect of developing and defining career alternatives is to begin the process of pulling together and reflecting on what you know about yourself. Turn back to the beginning of your notebook and slowly read through your material reflecting on your visioned vocation, keeping your visioned vocation in mind. What have you learned about yourself from your family history? Reflect on the should and ought messages given to you that are especially related to occupations. What are the needs that motivate you? Identify your native abilities in the area of data, people, ideas and things. What was learned from your work history and the tasks that you found satisfying and rewarding? How has your religious-belief-meaning system affected your occupational choice and development? Into what two major areas did your interests fall and thus your occupational focus? Skills and abilities in one field can be used in other fields. Many occupations are open to you. Is God's call pulling you to consider some specific areas?

The simplest way to gather information regarding the many and varied occupations available to you is to consult the *Dictionary of Occupational Titles* (DOT) put out by the United States Department of Labor. This book divides occupations into data, people and things. Focus on that area which already suits your basic abilities and interests. By reading through the listing you will be surprised at the many types of occupations available. A second volume that will also be helpful in gathering information regarding occupations is the *Occupational Outlook Handbook* also put out by the United States Department of Labor. Through these two volumes available in your library you can now begin to create a list of occupations that are of interest to you. Take your notebook and without evaluation or judgment begin to list vocations that will reflect who you are, what you believe, what your abilities and interests are, and your inner sense of God's call. Remember, at this point do not seek to evaluate the feasibility or practicality of any vocation that you list. It is important that you tap into your inner resources and gathered knowledge present in you through your imagination and dreams. For example, remember your childhood occupational dreams. Are they still with you? Over the years have you experienced a persistent pull to consider some dreamed-about work? God's call may be a persistent pull. God may speak to you through such things as curiosity, an idea, a feeling, repeated reminders, dreams or in other ways that draw attention to a need or a mission. Listen. Direct use of your active imagination can be a very productive access to vocation. For example, if you are a female, what kind of occupation can you imagine being available to you if you were male? If you are married, what occupations would you consider if you were not married? If money were no object, what would you do? If God spoke to you about your vocation, what would you hear? Using your information and imagination, write down as many possible vocations as you can think of. Take the time to do it now. Do not limit yourself to any specific number.

You are now ready to narrow the list. Probably the easiest way to narrow down the alternatives you have listed is to begin to eliminate. Eliminate those vocations which present immovable constraints and problems that cannot be overcome such as location, health requirements, and skills that would clearly be unattainable by you. Tap into your sense of values and eliminate those that clearly arouse a negative reaction. Eliminate those that are contrary to your own sense of God's calling. For you chemistry and math may indicate several career options such as working in the pharmaceutical field or working in the teaching field. Both options may be on your alternatives list but one is eliminated based upon your own sense of a commitment to the health of people and the welfare of people rather than the teaching of people. Cut this list as much as you can, remembering that you can always add alternatives to the list at a later time if you so desire. Second, now prioritize the remaining vocational options. First place those which are most satisfying and desirable at the top of your list. Next identify those which are satisfying and desirable and put them in a second list. Now put the remaining alternatives in a third list for those least satisfying and desirable. Eliminate those in list number three.

Now that you have narrowed the list to a reasonable size, it is time to gather specific information about each vocation on your list. Rank the list just developed in order of importance to you from one to twelve, with one being most important to you.

The kind of information that you would need to gather about each vocation is the vocational tasks, setting, training requirements, wages, benefits and how it fits in with your sense of God's call and mission as you understand it. There are a number of ways to gather information about a particular vocation. Gather printed material and read it. Look at any pre-packaged material that a company or group may put together about the vocation. One of the best ways to find out about a particular vocation is to talk to someone who is in that vocation. The object is to visit and talk with a person in the field and vocation in which you are especially interested. Call that person and make an appointment. By talking with someone personally you will get a first-hand knowledge of whether this particular vocation is a good fit for you. Ask the person what he or she does, what he or she likes about what he or she does, how he or she prepared for his or her vocation, what are the satisfactions and problems he or she experiences in his or her vocation? Bring your notebook with you and take notes during the interview so that you can reflect on them later. Most people are happy to tell you about what they do. Remember: the task at this time is to gather as much information as possible about a selected number of vocational choices that fit your basic abilities, interests, personality, religious-belief meaning system and sense of vocation.

As you complete this step you will realize that you know a great deal about yourself and about specific vocational choices. You are now ready to move on to choosing from among these alternatives a targeted vocation. This will be the focus of the next chapter. After targeting your vocation you will then move into the last two steps of career work, planning and marketing.

Chapter 4

Vocational Targeting

Step Three: Choosing a Vocation

This third step is critical. You have reached the step of choosing. In the last chapter you worked through, reflected and meditated on your career alternatives. Now you have reached the pivotal step in which you will evaluate the options and career alternatives open to you in order to arrive at a vocational choice. This choice will reflect where you are now. The choice of a vocation is, in fact, a developing process that unfolds over a period of time. To make a choice at this point is to center down into an area that you know is a good, reasonable and meaningful career direction for you at this time—a choice that reflects your present understanding of God's call. Vocational choices are made at specific times in our lives. However, vocational development and the on-going vocational conversation with God is a lifelong process. This process is ever sensitive and responsive to the many changes experienced in a lifetime. Frank, for example, responded to God's call early in his adult life by becoming a high school science teacher. By the time he reached thirty-five he felt pulled to law. He was deeply influenced by the break-up of several families of his students and the effects that the divorce had on their lives, particularly the custody hearings. After completing law school and becoming a lawyer he found much of law to be nitpicking and removed from people. After several years in a large law firm, he realized that he was called to work with adolescents. After much reflection, prayer and discussion with family and colleagues, he opened his own law firm specializing in working with adolescents. At the age of forty-eight he feels that the decisions and turns in his life were God's leading hand directing him to this vocation. He knows that this is where he needs to be at this time and reports that he will seek to be patient and open to any next step in his developing vocational career.

Given all the information and thought that has gone into choosing a vocation, a decision sounds like the easy step. For most of us it is difficult. The difficulty is the psychological aspects rather than the technical aspects of decision making. Strange as it may seem, people sometimes turn away from a decision for growth. They may resist taking a step toward what appears to be from the observers' perspective a reasonable, clear and helpful decision. Many people resist claiming their potential and moving toward actualization. A step for change may produce anxiety and fears. As you think about making a decision you may be aware of fears, doubts and reasons why you can't make a clear vocational decision.

One of the most common barriers to good decision making is fear. Every decision involves risks and thus fear. Many decisions involve going contrary to all we were told about ourselves and our world as we grew up. For example, Carol's mother told her that she was a "bad girl" if she asked for what she wanted. At the age of forty-two she is still afraid to ask for what she wants. She is hoping that her boss will see that she is a hard worker and thus worthy of becoming a department head. She has the abilities to do it but never speaks up when a department head position becomes available. An old irrational fear stops her movement toward a reasonable vocational choice. Choices are often met by fear. We are motivated by two powerful forces; one is fear and the other is desire. Each pushes us in opposite directions. They both, however, represent the opposite sides of the same coin. The opposite side of our fears is our desires and the opposite side of our desires is our fears. On the one hand, we may be motivated and pushed by the desire to move toward a new self-actualizing meaningful vocational choice. On the other side, we can get blocked by the opposite force of the fears of "I can't," "I won't" or "I mustn't." For example, Jean who grew up in eastern Pennsylvania and whose parents lived and worked within twenty-five miles of their parents' home had an outstanding job offer in California. She took the job but only stayed several months because of the inner fear of moving so far away from the family. Everyone seemed supportive to her but she knew deep inside her that she "shouldn't" move that far away, and so she couldn't. She did manage to find a job closer to home at a lesser salary with little challenge. Her fear, unspoken, blocked what appeared both to her and to others to be the right vocational choice.

Take some time now to reflect on your "I can'ts." What are those messages that are motivated by inner fears and stand as blocks to your choosing your targeted visualized vocation? Write down in column format on the left margin your "I can'ts."

Figure #3

I CAN'T	I CAN

Reflect on your "I can'ts" and decide which ones you want to change. Now go ahead and write next to each "I can't" an "I can." "I can'ts" in one list can be converted and changed into "I can" in your desire list. All fears can and may be changed into desires. Thus the motivating statement "I can't because I am afraid of failing" can be changed to the motivating force of desire "I can succeed."

For example:

I CAN'T	I CAN
move to another area	explore other areas to live
tell people my abilities	claim my abilities and let others know about them
move out of my parents' home	be my own person and live in my own place
go back to school	look at what is required and go back to school

Not only do we have to face the "I can'ts" in ourselves and the fears that push us away from our desires, but so often those around us tell us, "You can't." As you move toward your targeted vocation and consider carefully and precisely the choosing of that vocation, other people's expectations are sometimes supportive and sometimes negating. Claude, for example, in order to test out his choice of vocation, mentioned it to several of his friends in passing only to hear their surprise and objections, with such comments as "You can't do that—why bother?" or "No one in your family has ever done that." Such statements from people who are important to you become powerful barriers to your making a decision and acting on it. Are there such forces in your life? Take a moment to list your top three possible vocational goals. Then write beside each one how you think your parents, your best friend and an important person in your life would respond to such a goal. (See Figure #4) Naturally, other people will be quick to give you advice and to tell you what they think is the best thing for your life. However, clearly, you are in charge of your own life. You must choose what vocation best fits your needs and your understanding of God's call.

What is important is that you act. No matter how small or insig-

Figure #4

RESPONSE OF

VOCATIONAL GOAL	PARENTS	FRIENDS	IMPORTANT PERSON

nificant at the start, a step needs to be taken in the direction you want to go. You do not have to have all of the answers or have everything worked out completely in order to make a decision. You must choose to act on behalf of what you feel, sense or think will bring happiness and will move you toward self-actualization through vocation. However, do not minimize the power of your own and other people's fears, resistances and anxieties to block your actions. Given fears, anxieties and resistances, move to make a decision. Decide for your vocation.

To assist you further the next four exercises are designed to help you evaluate your visioned vocation and make a decision.

Desired Outcome Exercise[1]

The purpose of this exercise is to help you assess whether a particular vocational choice will help you meet your desired goals. The exercise seeks to answer the question, "How likely is each vocational option to provide my desired outcome?" Each of us has desired goals, expected outcomes from our vocational life. These goals might include such things as money, job security, community, working alone, a desire to teach people, a desire to be in charge, etc. Reflect on your desired goals. Then take a few minutes to list them in your notebook. This list becomes the desired outcome goals from your vocation. Be as specific as possible.

Now select from your list of desired goals the top six and list them on a new page in priority order from one to six with one your preferred first outcome. Across the top of the page list your preferred vocations. (Figure 5) In this way each vocation has a column under it.

If you have more than three or four options use more pages. Take one option at a time and estimate the likelihood of that option providing your desired outcomes. Give a numerical value to each: three equals very likely, two equals somewhat likely, and one equals unlikely. The scoring is based on your perception of how each vocation will meet your desired goals. No one can determine the numerical value but you. If you need further information about a particular vocation and how well it meets your desired outcome, then ask someone in the vocation or consult the *Occupational Outlook Handbook*. For example, you may not know what the average salary is of your vocational option. The Handbook will give you that information.

How likely is each option to provide the desired outcome?

       3 = very likely   2 = somewhat likely   1 = unlikely

Figure #5

Vocational Options

Desired Outcomes					

TOTALS

For example:

desired outcomes	vocational options		
	social worker	minister	high school teacher
job security	2	3	2
money	2	1	3
use creativity	1	3	3
serve people	3	3	2
status	1	2	2
autonomy	2	3	2
TOTAL	11	15	14

In our example found in Figure #5A above, the numerical values are based on the person's own personal value system and the reality of the job market. When you have completed each column, then total up the score in each and you should be able to see at a glance how your options compare. In Figure #5A based on the desired options and the person's valuing those options, the ministry followed by high school teaching and then social worker are the priority list. It is important to remember that these numbers are measured against your desired outcome, what you want from your vocation. This first exercise should give you some very helpful information for decision making.

Pro and Con Exercise[2]

The purpose of this exercise is to help you consider the long and short term advantages and disadvantages of each vocational option. Short term usually means within the next six months or within a shorter period of time. Long term usually means over a five or ten year period. Take one page for each vocational option. List the option at the top of the page. Divide the page into two parts—the top part for short term and the bottom part for long term. Now divide the page lengthwise into two sides—one side for "Pro," advantages, and the other side for "Con," disadvantages. Fill in each quadrant in any order, making sure all are filled. What are the advantages and disadvantages of this vocational option for the short term and for the long term? Since most vocational options have both pros and cons, consider each carefully. Do this for each vocational option. It will be helpful to repeat this exercise several times, with each option becoming more and more specific.

Figure #6

Vocational Option: _____

PRO ADVANTAGES	CON DISADVANTAGES
SHORT TERM	
LONG TERM	

This exercise will help you reflect on each option and give you vital information for your final decision making.

Reflection on "Call" Exercise

The purpose of this exercise is to measure your vocational options against the criteria for understanding God's "call." In your notebook take a separate page for each vocational option and note the option at the top of the page. For each option ask yourself the following questions:

1. Can I serve God in this vocation?
2. Can I serve my neighbor in this vocation?
3. Is this vocation in harmony with my faith?
4. Will this vocation use and enhance my natural abilities?

It is clear that for the Christian, vocation never violates God's law. The commandments to love God and to love neighbor and to love yourself are closely and inseparably intertwined with vocation. Reflect on your answers. When the work that we do is congruent and in harmony with what we believe, then we experience a sense of movement toward self-fulfillment, self-actualization, and away from egocentricity. Vocation requires a centered ego, not an ego-centered life. God has given every one of us at least one talent and expects that we will use that talent as good stewards with people and creation. God does not want us to waste our talent or hide it, but does require at some point an accounting.

Both the Old Testament's and the New Testament's understanding of vocation gives us clear criteria for recognizing God's call in vocation.

1. Vocation is directed toward a particular task or mission.
2. The person called will receive for his or her fidelity to vocation some kind of reward both in this life where the person is promised intimate union with God and especially in the next where he or she is promised to be with God in "paradise."
3. The element which appears most frequently in vocation is the promise and the assurance of God's protection and assistance guaranteeing the success of the vocation and mission entrusted to us.
4. Vocation includes above all a total commitment of the self, the mind, body and spirit to that targeted vocation and thus will mean

and demand some renunciation of those parts of the self and the world that become barriers to this vocation.

Do your vocational options meet these criteria?

As you seek to understand God's call it is important for you to ask for help in discerning, understanding, accepting and committing yourself to that choice. On-going prayer and meditation are assumed. They are vital parts of this process toward your vocational decision.

Future Forecast Exercise

This exercise seeks to pull together in a guided fantasy the material in the previous exercises. Guided fantasy and imagination play a vital role in career planning and development.[3] In many ways guided fantasy resembles some forms of meditation. The purpose of a guided fantasy is to help you tap into your vast inner resources stored in the subconscious mind. One of the unique strengths of this exercise is that it shifts you from a predominant left brain mode to a right brain mode. Left brain and right brain are parallel ways of knowing. We need both. The left brain way of knowing is analytic, symbolic, abstract, verbal, rational, digital, logical and linear. Right brain way of knowing is synthetic, concrete, analogic, non-verbal, non-rational, spatial, intuitive and holistic.[4] Most of us have been trained to be predominantly left brain knowledge gatherers. One of the marvelous capabilities of the right brain is imagining, that is, seeing an imaginary picture with your mind's eye. When you combine this with the inner resources found in the subconscious mind, then you have a marvelous way of pulling together the vast amount of information you have gathered. The subconscious mind is the extensive library of the mind that stores for our use all the events, experiences, facts and information we ever experienced. This private extensive library like a vast number of computer disks can be tapped into and the information available to us at a moment's notice. One of the ways you can tap into this library of the subconscious mind is through guided fantasy. You can draw from your library facts and experiences and form these opinions and sort through these opinions to develop solutions, directions and actions that can direct your life. This is what makes guided fantasy and imagination so helpful in career planning and development.

The following is a suggested guided fantasy. You may choose to read the instructions over carefully and then follow them as you remember them. Second, you may ask a friend to read the instructions to you at a relaxed slow pace. Third, you may choose to read the instructions into a tape recorder and then play them back to yourself. Whichever method you decide to use, it is important that the guided fantasy be read and presented at a relaxed slow pace. When you use this guided fantasy, sit in a relaxing chair, close your eyes and take deep relaxing breaths. Follow the fantasy journey in your imagination.

> Find a comfortable place to sit, placing your hands at your side and both feet on the floor . . . take a deep breath, not so deep that it is uncomfortable but deep enough that you can relax . . . close your eyes and let yourself go slowly into a deep relaxing place . . . breathe deeply and relax . . .
>
> Now let your imagination take you forward in time. Just let any images come to your mind. You do not need to answer any questions aloud, just let the images form. Come with me now to the future. One year . . . (give the date of the year if you wish) . . . two years . . . three years . . . relax as you move to the fourth year and slowly to year number five . . . relax, it is comfortable here and you will feel relaxed and refreshed.
>
> It is morning; you are just awakening from a deep sleep in your imagination. You are lying in bed just a minute longer before getting up and doing the things that you usually do before breakfast. Become aware of your surroundings . . . your room. Do you live in a city, a town, a farm, a house or an apartment? . . . Notice how your room is decorated? Are you alone? . . . Now get up and get dressed for work. This is the vocation you have been looking for that brings satisfaction and joy. As you dress for your vocation, become aware of what you are wearing.
>
> On your way to breakfast now, look around you . . . feel good about your home. What is this place like? See if there is anyone with you. Eat breakfast now and notice how good you feel about yourself.
>
> It is time to go to work . . . perhaps you will stay and work at home or perhaps you will leave. If you leave, notice the

Vocational Targeting

route you travel. Do you walk? . . . drive? . . . take public transportation? train or a bus? How do things look along the way? Do you see anyone you know?

You are approaching where you work if you are not already there. What do you notice? What do you feel as you enter and start doing your work? Do you have a title? Let yourself experience this vocation. Be aware of what you are doing . . . Who else is there? What are they doing? Feel good about this work. Complete your morning work right up to your lunch time.

It's lunch time now. Do you stay in or go out for lunch? Do you eat with friends or alone?

Return to work now and finish your work day. You are aware that this is the vocation you are called to do . . . See if anything is different in the afternoon.

When you have completed work leave your place of business or office. Feel good about yourself . . . Return to where you live. See what you notice along the way home. Enjoy your evening meal . . . In the evening imagine feeling good about your day and rewarding yourself. When you go to bed you know that this has been a very satisfying and rewarding day. You have a clear view of your vocation.

Imagine yourself returning to the fourth year . . . (give the date of the year if you wish) . . . three years . . . two years and returning to the present . . .

You are awakening now, refreshed, renewed, opening your eyes and sitting in your seat . . . aware, sensitive and knowledgeable about the experience you have just completed. Open your eyes now and be fully awake.

Take a moment to relax and let the experience be absorbed. Now record the experience in your notebook.
This experience allowed you to be in contact with the inner imaginative, creative part of the self that is usually overlooked. You have tapped into your inner reservoir of wisdom and knowledge available through the right brain.

You may discover that this guided fantasy may reveal the same or a different vocation from the one with which you initially began this journey. By now your vocational direction may be very clear, obvious, and a decision may be easy. For others it may not be so obvious and you may need to let the information gathered simmer in your subconscious, knowing that you may be able to make the decision the next morning or within a week. For some it is important to let the inner guiding presence of God persistently pull you toward the correct decision. In the final analysis, the only instruction that can be given is decide. Decide! Then complete the statement, THE VOCATION I PLAN TO PURSUE IS _____ .

You are now ready for the launching steps.

Step Four: Making a Plan

Now that you have made a vocational choice, the next step is to make a plan which will give you your own individual map to accomplish your vocational goal. This map will be a step by step course to follow in order to actualize that which you have seen and experienced as potential. This is not a difficult step but one that is very important. As the old adage states, "If you fail to plan, you plan to fail." You know where you want to go; now plan how you are going to get there.

The best plan and the easiest to put together is a straight line plan in which sequential steps are presented. The line may follow a time line sequence. For example, what dates and months will specific steps be accomplished? Peter sees his vocational goal taking three years to reach. He will place the month and year by each specific step needed to reach the goals in three years. Other straight line plans follow a task line sequence such as listing the specific tasks to be accomplished without noting a month or year. With this task line Peter would list each specific task needed to accomplish his goal whether it takes three years or five years. Most people use a combination of both time and task lines. In this way Peter would note carefully the specific tasks and beside each task give a month and year for its accomplishment.

You can write down your own individual plan in your notebook. It is most helpful to begin with the end, where you want to be, and work backward to now. Write down your vocational goal. This is the end of your task and time line. Now list the steps necessary to accomplish this goal. Write these down in sequential order. Linda, whose vocational goal is to teach high school English, can work backward from there to accepting the job, job interviewing, sending out resumes, preparing resumes, graduating from college, talking to her college advisor to be sure she has the right courses. Now write the list again, reversing the order and beginning with the present task and moving to the future goal. As you do this make sure you did not forget any step. In rewriting her list Linda wrote: talking to her college advisor to be sure she had the right courses (she had to add courses), graduating from college, preparing a resume. She then added: preparing a cover letter to send out with each resume, job interviewing, and accepting the job teaching high school English.

Go through your plan and begin to identify the sub-steps needed. When you have completed this, add reasonable dates at each step along the way to your goal.

Your plan ought to be seen as a guide and not as a rigid path from which you cannot deviate. All plans run into snags, blocks and changes as you begin to progress through them. You will find yours. Your plan also will need to be flexible, changeable and evaluated after the accomplishment of each step, much like playing a game of chess. The goal of the chess game is very clear and that is to checkmate your opponent's king. After each move is made the situation is evaluated and the next move is planned. When that move is made the situation is again evaluated and the next move replanned. So it is with the planning and replanning of your steps toward your vocational goal.

Many things will affect your plan. The execution of that plan will depend upon the feasibility and the skills that you have to carry out the various steps. It becomes very important for you to evaluate each step. Ask yourself several questions at each step. First, can this be done? In other words, can that step be accomplished at this particular time, in this particular place, with my particular resources? Second, can I do it successfully? Here again, it requires your taking a look at your own resources and situation. Third, what are the constraints? Fourth, what are the resources you bring to this step? In this way you will be able to identify the barriers that may occur at each step. As you consider each step list those barriers of which you are aware. What are the barriers to the action needed to accomplish this step? Next to each barrier list the actions that you need to take to break that barrier and move through that step to the next step in your plan.

Now you are ready to work your plan.

Step Five: The Vocational Search

There is a difference between doing the job, keeping the job and getting the job. This fifth step is built upon the self-understanding that you can do the job, you can keep the job, and now you have to get the job. Getting a job involves an effective vocational search. The search is based upon your self-understanding and your commitment to the vocation. It is based upon your understanding of your abilities and talents to do that job and your sense of God's calling which makes the occupation a vocation.

There are some who would say that at this point you must let God do it. You need simply to wait quietly and passively till people have the good sense to see how bright and well motivated you are, how skilled you are, and that God wants you to have the job which they have available. If you wait and let God open the door, then it certainly will be the job God wants you to do. For some people this may work for them. You cannot rule out God's guiding hand in your vocational search. The fact is that you are seeking to invite God into your search. I firmly believe that God will be with you in your vocational search. However, you need to take an active part in the search knowing that God is with you. Getting that vocation as the response to God's call is a joint search. Your part is to conduct an excellent vocational search. This search will entail hard work, time, commitment and a clear understanding that this is the vocation for you. You will need to continually invite God's presence, guidance and support into this vocational search. To go on from this point without walking with God is to set aside all that you have done so far to invite God's call to direct you to the most reasonable and meaningful response in vocation.

Most employers want a resume. A resume is your self-marketing presentation. It is a written summary of your personal, educational, and experience qualifications intended to demonstrate your fitness for a particular position. The purpose of the resume is to open the door for careers other than entry level positions. The resume is usually accompanied by a specific letter of application and is sent directly to the employer. Its intent is to draw attention to who you are and what you have to offer to that particular employer. Therefore, the resume should package your qualifications in an appealing wrapper so that the employer will not pass it up. There are a number of books that have been written on putting together a resume. It would be helpful to consult one or more for a more in-depth look at the subject.

Briefly stated, a resume should tell the future employer: first, who you are (identification information), second, what you want to do (occupation objective), and, third, what you have to offer in the way of education, experience, and personal experience (background information). Writing the resume gives you a good opportunity to pull together in specific form what you know about you, and what your gifts are. Writing a resume is similar to reflecting on and composing an advertisement, stating clearly who you are, what you want and what it is you especially bring to the vocation. You may find it helpful to write the material in an informal fashion at first, then review it. Then let those important persons in your life read it and help you reflect on it. After gathering and writing this informal material you are ready to write your resume.

L.W. Schrank has summarized in her book some helpful rules for writing a resume.[5]

1. Write short, concise sentences. Use as few words as necessary to express your accomplishments.
2. Use action verbs to begin each sentence or phrase. Examples: created, exhibited, mobilized, repaired, designed, motivated, presented.
3. Use the vocabulary or "jargon" of your field, but avoid becoming overly technical. Speak a language the person reading the resume will understand.
4. List specific accomplishments and results. Use numbers when possible, e.g. increased production by twenty-five percent, won Atlantic Monthly National Short Story writing contest, devised sales campaign that netted $15,000 for class treasury.
5. Convey one selling point at a time; don't confuse your accomplishments by grouping too many ideas together.
6. Put the concerns of your potential employer ahead of your own needs. This may mean not specifying in the resume desired salary.
7. Don't get too personal; you do not need to include your picture in your resume.
8. Type the resume in clear, clean typeface; the layout should look professional and encourage people to read it. Retain sufficient white space, leaving at least one inch margins, double space between paragraphs.
9. Fit your resume on one page of $8\frac{1}{2} \times 11$ inch paper.

Employers receive many resumes each week and often spend as little time as fifteen seconds on each one.
10. Have someone proofread your final copy for any mistakes.
11. Have the resume professionally printed. (Photo-offset is best.) Select off-white, beige or light gray paper, heavy grade quality. Buy from the printer matching envelopes and blank pieces of paper for writing your cover letter.

It is important to remember that your resume is your self-marketing advertisement. You are your own best advertising manager and your task at this point is to sell yourself.

If you send your resume through the mail in responding to a job advertisement in the newspaper or a want-ad notice, then you should send a cover letter with your resume. The purpose of the cover letter is to invite the prospective employer to read with more interest your resume. The cover letter should speak more specifically to the job advertised as available and to your specific interests, qualifications and availability for the position.

It is time now for action. The trickiest part of securing a vocation is finding leads that will result in an offer. The United States Department of Labor surveyed ten million job seekers about how they set up interviews that resulted in a job offer. The most effective method for every occupation (except clerical) was applying directly to the employer. Answering newspaper ads came in second, while private employment agencies came in third. Twelve percent of the interviews resulted from employment agency contacts, twenty-one percent from advertising, and a whopping sixty-seven percent from direct negotiation between employer and candidate or other initiatives of the candidate.[6]

In light of the above statistics, one method that has an excellent success rate in securing a vocation is to use an advice and information interview. An advice and information interview is an interview with someone in your desired vocational field. The purpose of this interview is to gather information and advice regarding your focused vocation. The point is to ask for information and advice and not to ask for a job. You must keep this perfectly clear. At this interview you are trying to find out what people do in their work, how that fits your visioned vocation. Job offers grow out of advice and information interviews but are not the focus of the interview. Advice and information interviews are an excellent way for you to be introduced to

Vocational Targeting

the specifics in your vocational field. Since so many occupations are not advertised and are secured through personal contact and referral, it is extremely important that you meet the people in the field. It will give you a chance to see if this vocation really fits you. You will be asking another person to look at you and give you his or her ideas about how he or she sees you fitting into the vocation. You will be asking another person to brainstorm with you about where you fit in that vocational field. Remember, an advice and information interview is not a job interview but a very important opportunity to get to know the field and be known by those working in the job. The advice and information interview is a vital step in entering the vocation especially in light of the fact that roughly seventy-five to eighty percent of non-entry level jobs are not made known publicly.

Begin your interviews. Find someone in your focused vocation and ask him or her for an interview. You may already know somebody in the field. This person may be a friend, a family member, a fellow church member or someone you were introduced to at a party. It is helpful to make a list of persons you know or that other family members may know and could introduce you. You may need to go to the Yellow Pages and randomly select a company or group. Call and ask to speak with the personnel manager or to the person doing the type of work in which you are interested.

Begin your calls. Make it very clear that you are not asking for a job, only information and advice, and that you need only fifteen or twenty minutes of their time. If they agree to talk they may give you more time. People like to talk about what they do and how they got into their vocation. If you are presently employed, tell them that and that you don't need a job, only information and advice. Set up a time. Be punctual. Remember, they are doing you a favor, so be appreciative.

The interview should include information about them and their work and about you, your skills and special knowledges. Ask questions such as:

- What do you do during your day?
- What do you like most about your vocation? least?
- Where do you see your field going in the future?
- What skills are necessary for this type of vocation?
- Share with them your skills and special knowledges.
- Ask if you might fit in that vocation.
- What challenges and problems do you see ahead for you?
- What is the salary range for this type of vocation?
- What does the future look like for employment in the vocation?

Since you have already gathered information about this vocation, you may wish to ask additional questions from your reading. If you start your interview in a general way, you should be able to get more specific as the interview progresses. It will be very helpful to hear this person's advice about how you might do in the vocation after you share your skills and abilities. Ask him or her if you might fit in the vocation, then seek to find out how he or she got his or her job. Before the interview ends and you are thinking of leaving, be sure to ask the person if there is another person in the field that he or she could recommend with whom you should speak. In this way you will be able to build a network of interviews using recommended people in the field.

After the interview it is important that you take the time to put down the person's name, phone number, address, etc. Especially note in your notebook what you learned during the interview. You may want to use this information later. It is better not to write during the interview. Concentrate on developing an ally, a friend and a relationship; then follow up immediately with a thank you note. If you have received any leads for further interviews, follow up with them and let the person know who referred you. This will help you and him or her make a smoother transition to the next interview. It is important that you listen. Particularly listen for problems. Remember that people hire to help them solve problems. You may be the very person they need.

Jobs come out of these advice and information interviews. You may be offered a job during the process. Think carefully. Remember, this is not a job interview and that was not the purpose of the interview. Don't jump impulsively. Thank the person and tell him or her that you are flattered and that you will go home, think about it, and call him or her back to set up an interview to discuss the job. Then set up a job interview and focus on all the specific questions and issues you need to know before accepting an offer.

The job interview is the single most important step in securing your vocation. It is your opportunity to present your abilities, your skills and yourself in a confident and clear manner. It is also your opportunity to determine if you want to work for this company or employer. The interview is a mutual venture in which both you and the employer need to negotiate. They have something you need and you have something they need. Therefore, think of the interview as a negotiation where the basic issues are: What do I want? What do you want? How can we both get what we want? During the interview communicate directly, honestly and assertively. Some people are assertive, some non-assertive and some aggressive during an interview. The most successful are assertive.[7] Non-assertive people are often apologetic, self-effacing and have a poor sense of self-esteem during the interview. They communicate through their words and behavior: "I don't count. You really shouldn't hire me. My feelings don't matter, only yours do. I'm nothing. You're superior." These people tend to fiddle with glasses and jewelry, may cover their mouths when they speak, direct their eyes down and blink rapidly. They sometimes smile and laugh inappropriately as a result of their inner stress and the internal message of poor self-worth.

Aggressive people on the other hand stand up for their rights, thoughts, feelings and beliefs even if it means attacking others. They tend to dominate to get their point across. Their message to the employer is: "I must win; you are unimportant. I'm superior and my thoughts and feelings matter more than yours." They often express themselves through rapid speech, condescending manner, pointing fingers, hands on the hips, a bored expression and tight-lipped speech.

Assertive behavior in an interview is the best way to present yourself and your rights to claim your vocation. Assertive people believe in their basic human rights. They approach others as human beings, not adversaries or objects. They stand up for their rights, needs, desires and beliefs because they are very aware of their own natural child. They articulate their thoughts honestly and directly without violating other people's rights. These persons use direct eye contact. They are open, relaxed in their facial expression, firm with their voice, and present a relaxed demeanor. The assertive person communicates: "I'm O.K. and so are you."

In preparing for your interview be aware of how you are presenting yourself. Be assertive in both your verbal and non-verbal presentation. This means being clear about who you are and what you want from life and your vocation. The sense of certainty grows out of your awareness that God does have a mission for you and that this is your way of responding to that call in vocation. This ought not to be presented in a manner that gives the other the message that you are somehow better or more religious than he or she because you are seeking to respond to God's call. This was always the dilemma of the Hebrew people in the Old Testament. In order for them to fulfill their call they had to recognize that the call was to service and not to superiority over another. Our call too is to servanthood and not to superiority. With vocation comes the realization that this is not simply a job but rather a response to God's call and as such invites God to be with you through this interview process. You must do your part; then you will know that God is with you. This affirmation brings both self-confidence and the strength to be assertive.

Go prepared for your interview. This means claiming both your call and your abilities. It means taking the time to study and to become familiar with the work of the business or company you are interviewing. The interviewer will want to know about you, your personality. They thus want to know, "Can you get along with others and add a positive dimension to the company?" Second, they will want to know your employment history and expectations. They are interested in how much you are committed to this vocation and what you will contribute to this company. Third, they will want to talk about salary and benefits. You should be aware of what a realistic salary range is for this particular vocation. This can be done by doing some research and answering the questions: What is the highest salary you could earn? What is the lowest dollar amount you would accept for this work? Since there are many factors that enter into a salary package it is important that you review your information gathered at the advice and information interview as a helpful basis. What is reasonable can be discussed with family and friends and verified through state employment offices and the *Occupational Outlook Handbook*. Sometimes a careful and thorough review of newspapers, trade journals and other companies will be helpful. You should be prepared in the interview to ask questions about not only the job and the company, but also the salary range, responsibilities, benefits and opportunities for advancement.

Some suggestions that will help make your interview go smoother are:

- Be punctual.
- Act naturally and courteously.
- Dress in business-like clothing. Ask yourself "What do successful people in this line of work wear?" and dress accordingly.
- Listen to the questions carefully, taking a few seconds to think about your answer. Answer clearly and concisely. Do not exaggerate your abilities or experience.
- Respond to all questions. If it is helpful to you, volunteer information which might concern the interviewer but cannot be legally asked.
- Remember to use the name of the interviewer.
- Maintain a posture of interest. Establish eye contact with the interviewer.

- Be prepared with questions about the job and the company that you are entitled to know.
- Be prepared with credentials and references.
- Be enthusiastic and self-confident.
- Do not criticize yourself or other people.
- Avoid wisecracks.
- Do not smoke unless the interviewer is smoking.
- Be sure to thank the interviewer at the end of the interview.[8]

Remember that you may need more than one interview. Many employers use two or more interviews as a way of narrowing down the field of potential candidates. They are also interested in whether you are consistent over several interviews. Being yourself and inviting God's presence into the interview process will be very helpful in keeping the patience, insight and confidence in a good perspective over what might be several weeks or months. Do not lose sight of your focused vocation and God's call. Sometimes not getting the job with one company or firm may leave you free to accept a better opportunity later. Since you have invited God into this process through prayer and meditation it is important to listen and be continually in conversation with God's leading. Is this the vocation that truly responds to God's call, or is this an ego-serving trip on my part? You have worked hard to get to this place; now is the time to remain alert and patient to the leading of God.

Celebrate when the vocation is in hand. Recognize that this is the beginning of a new and exciting journey. As you have gone through this process it is essential that you move toward that vocation which balances your abilities, gifts and talents with God's call and mission.

Life continues to change. Our understanding of God's call grows and changes. Our personal and family needs change. The economy and political climate we live in change. Remember that from time to time you will want to assess your skills and interests. You will want to develop new skills and use them to move into new areas. With these changes will come the need to reassess and recommit yourself to vocation. You are involved in a lifelong conversation with God about vocation in the midst of continual change. The fidelity to the conversation about vocation makes it possible for you to take the changes in stride and to take the steps of your journey with confidence. Change will happen, and there is no need for it to throw you. It is part of God's plan that we grow through change. Make the time of change a time of growth for you. Change in one area of your life such as marriage, children, death of a loved one, or physical illness will necessitate a re-evaluation of your vocational commitment. For instance, after several years in your first vocation with the developing family and children issues, or if you are single, with the continuing reflection and adjustment to the single life, you will want to consider where you are in your vocation. Mid-life and pre-retirement are two other areas that invite us to reconsider our vocational direction.

The experiences and information gathered in this career/vocational process will become the bottom line upon which you can build and grow in vocational career development. Career development and the career counseling that is involved is not a once event but rather a repeated experience at the various transition points in life. Thus career development and the counseling involved is a normative experience oriented toward growth, health and vocational wellness rather than toward vocational problems. Vocational problems will occur, and at times you will certainly seek career counseling. However, career counseling is not simply for the vocationally troubled. It is also for those times of normal transition. It is part of the on-going developmental process of each person's movement toward continual vocational response to God's call.

Chapter 5

Career Development

Adult life is an on-going, dynamic flowing process like a stream ever moving toward the sea, not a stagnant, stable experience like a pool of water trapped in the depression of a field. This continuous development of each person results from multiple influences of biology, psychology, and environmental determinants. Childhood development, for instance, focuses primarily on the formation of the psychic structure and the self. Adult development is concerned with the continual evolution of that existing psyche and self-structure and with its involvement with others in love and work. The on-going process invites change whether we want it or not. Changes are rarely smooth and may be seen at various points as crises. A crisis is a dangerous opportunity. There are thus varying degrees of stress and strain and crises throughout adult life, and how we respond to them as adults requires our personal adaptation, flexibility, insight and understanding of God's involvement which brings meaning and purpose to our life changes. These normative crises or transitions become the dominant theme in our adult development. Transitions are events or non-events that require a corresponding change in our behavior, our relationships or our self-understanding. Transitions are part of our adult development and include changes in such areas as our values, our world views, and our personal appearance. Adult life may be deeply influenced by body and physical changes. No one escapes these personal transitions, and how we approach them, deal with them, and understand them depends on whether we experience them as painful life adjustments or opportunities for personal growth. It is important to note that there are a wide variety of individual personal and group differences in life, and therefore there are a variety and wide range of responses based on gender, race and culture. It cannot be emphasized too strongly that even though we can identify a series of developmental and transitional stages that adults go through, individuals respond to each stage and at each transition uniquely and differently, based on who they are, how they are experiencing life, and how they experience God's intervention to bring meaning and direction to the adult normative transition stages.

Erik Erikson in his work has given us a helpful overview of three stages in adult development. The first one he calls early adulthood, from approximately age twenty to age thirty-five. He notes that this is the stage of acquiring a sense of identity and the avoidance of a sense of isolation. The second stage he calls middle adulthood, approximately age thirty-five to sixty-five. Here the task is of acquiring a sense of generativity and avoiding a sense of stagnation. The third stage he calls late adulthood, found at the approximate age of sixty-five. The task is acquiring a sense of integrity and fending off a sense of despair. The process of development through adulthood is not simply an unfolding of maturational potentials from within nor simply an adult socialization system. Rather the fundamental issues of childhood do continue to be central aspects of adult life but experienced in a different form and in a different way. As individuals grow older, they work to eliminate childhood distortions that restrict and distort their full enjoyment of adulthood. The issues of childhood live on into adulthood as the inner child of the past. Thus self-assessment, self-understanding and the continual process of eliminating childhood distortions are critical to the on-going adult issues of love and work.

Work is a central issue in the lives of most adults. Work is an essential part of being alive. For many people work is closely tied to the sense of identity and self-esteem. What we do at work tells us often who we are. This is easy to understand when we consider the lengthy period of time that adults devote to work—forty to fifty hours a week for thirty to fifty years of their life. Some people become involved in work because of what work can provide for them: a new house, a car, a vacation. It is not the work itself that is important but rather the money that is earned in work that is important. To many others, work itself is what is important. It contributes to the sense of self-esteem and worth, and has the experience of bringing joy in doing the work. In this sense, work now begins to move toward a vocation. Work as it contributes to self-esteem helps us know visibly that we can be efficient and competent in dealing with the tasks of a job. We acquire a sense of control over both ourselves and our environment by accomplishing such a task. Work also contributes to our sense of self-esteem in that we produce something when working that is valued by ourselves or by others. This can make us feel worthwhile as persons.

Career development is the on-going, dynamic development of the work aspect of our life. Career development is only one aspect of individual development. Like adult development itself it is not limited to one confined period of time but rather is a dynamic, flowing process through adult life, responsive to and informing the other aspects of our on-going development. Career development is a process lasting throughout adult life. It is related to the personality development and the on-going process of becoming a full actualized person through the elimination of childhood distortions and the tyrannies and sometimes painful messages given to us as children. Just as each period of adult development is filled with opportunities and crises, so each period is filled with significant opportunities and crises for vocation.

It is important to note that throughout this process there are depersonalizing forces that seek to change us as individuals within the world of work that would make us into persons who are simply operators, sellers or keepers. It is easy for us to drift into occupations that become treadmills and to experience a loss of personal meaning and joy in our work. The first thing that we need to be aware of is that we are unique individual persons with a richness of talents, gifts and abilities as children of God living in a world of things and as workers in that world. A second thought that we need to keep in mind is that God is very much a part of our world, and that he has a plan for what we are doing. When we are sensitive and responsive to God's call, then the work that we do in our vocation we are doing faithfully as God's work in the world. Like adult life itself, God's call is not a single event, but rather experienced differently at each turn and transition in our career development. As we begin to be aware and know when through our work we are faithful to God's call, we participate in God's on-going creative work in the world. Thus it cannot be said too strongly that for the person who seeks to bring work into a vocation, prayer and meditation are vital on-going parts of the process. There are times in which we will experience stress and pain and discouragement in our career development. However, our conversation with God is not just something we do at some times in our life but rather something we must commit ourselves to as part of an on-going life commitment. Whether we are twenty-five and seeking to make an early career decision or whether we are sixty and aware of our possible retirement and change in our sense of vocation, God is present. God calls us to vocation where we are.

Career development stages have been presented by a number of significant theorists in the field (Gould, Super, Levenson, Holland). The career development cycle is well documented. I would like to present the following flow and overview of life stages and development to be looked at in more detail in the balance of this chapter.

1. Late Adolescence—Ages Sixteen to Twenty-Two

This is the preparation stage where the late adolescent youth begins to leave the parents' world and seeks independence and preparation for the world of work. He or she is moving out of his or her parents' world, seeking more independence and preparing himself or herself to explore the possibilities of adult work and to test his or her choices.

2. Young Adulthood—Ages Twenty-Two to Twenty-Eight

This is the time of gaining the independence to work and to form other intimate relationships. It is the testing of parental messages. The task is getting started in an occupation. It is the time of securing one's first job and the initial work pursued after training or education.

3. The Thirties Transition—Ages Twenty-Eight Through Thirty-Two

This is a time of questioning the earlier commitments to work and relationships, career and marriage. It is a time of reassessment and possible change in vocation.

4. The Establishment Time—Ages Thirty-Two Through Thirty-Nine

This is the time of rooting, a time to deal with the establishment of vocation and family. It is often the last chance to have children and the time to demonstrate competency in and adjustment to one's vocation.

5. Mid-Life Transition—Ages Thirty-Nine Through Forty-Three

This is another opportunity for reappraisal, sometimes experienced as an unstable period of personal reassessment and discomfort. Persons reassess their earlier dreams which they may or may not have attained and begin to wonder where they are going and consider making radical lifestyle changes.

6. Restabilization Time—Ages Forty-Three Through Fifty

After the strain and stress and changes of the mid-life upheaval, it is followed by a general period of stabilization where a person begins to feel more settled. A new career may be entered into or the old career may begin to blossom. The person is now beginning to ask more and more questions of meaning. It is the time of advancement in one's vocational career and the solid establishment of it.

7. The Renewal Phase—Ages Fifty Through Sixty-Five

This is a time of relative calm, a time of experiencing the rewards of one's work, accepting and enjoyment of life and planning for retirement. Physical and emotional energies may begin to decline and new life patterns may begin to emerge. The anticipation of retirement begins to see the slowing down of work and decline in the workplace.

8. Retirement—Ages Sixty-Five and Up

This is considered to be the golden years when one begins to experience a new sense of usefulness to society and growth within oneself.

It is important to remember that these stages are based upon our social norms both past and present. Since our world is rapidly changing, so are its social norms—the norms and values and different people at different times and stages in their life.

Many of the studies done in the past have focused on male career development, and the sequence may not be the process experienced by many women. The career development cycles of women are often related to family. We begin to see a slightly different pattern for many women in career development. It is important to make special note of that before going on to look in more depth at these eight stages. More and more women are experiencing the same career development cycle that men experience as a flow from the late adolescence through the retirement phases. Other women experience a different career pattern. The reason for this is that women more than men face two major obstacles to developing themselves as a worker, maker or producer in our society. One is the mythologizing of the mother-homemaker role and at the same time its devaluation in the real world. The other is the failure of women to see work as a necessary component of identity and autonomy. Little girls, for example, are more likely to think of work as an adjunct to something else like relationships, motherhood, and homemaking. Women, more than men, seem to be caught in the tension between career and homemaking. Many women who enter the work force see work as a waiting time until they can establish a family, have children, and spend time in homemaking and parenting. Even college educated women usually only work for a few years until they start their families. Many women define their femininity in terms of successfully achieving the roles of marriage and motherhood. Self-esteem is developed through the marriage state for many women, as Madonna Kolbenschlag, in her book *Kiss Sleeping Beauty Goodbye*, notes: "Indeed for many women marriage and anticipated motherhood represents a release from a prison sentence: shackled to a nine to five job, a role perhaps characterized by monotony, powerlessness, and de-personalization. The role of mother-homemaker by contrast at least provides intimacy and a sense of personal power. Later the uneasiness will set in."[1]

The career development cycle for many women then involves the same late adolescent concerns and preparation, and, second, the young adult phase with a tension arising between continuing in one's career or taking on the occupation of family and motherhood. If the second is preferable, then it is usually not until the late thirties or mid-forties that women become uneasy and seek again to re-enter a vocation. They usually enter at the preparation stage and re-employment stage either through an academic or a vocational system. They enter a vocation in order to overcome the spiritual inertia, recover their sense of autonomy and identity, and, now that their children are leaving, re-enter the work world. At this point they begin again the career development cycle flowing through a preparation stage, an establishment stage, a maintenance stage and a retirement stage in a much condensed and abbreviated manner than their male counterparts.

There are certainly a number of complex factors that contribute to this. We must not rule out the biological factor. Van Hoose in his book notes that for single women who need to succeed and achieve in a career, the first ten years after college graduation find their achievement motivation showing a noticeable decline. Fifteen years after graduation these same persons saw an increase in their motivation to achieve. For the twenty to twenty-five year period after graduation from college the achievement motivation was extremely high and stable. He notes that the level of achievement motivation was found to be correlated to the ages of child-bearing. The drive was low when children were born and were young, moderate when no children were planned, and high once child-bearing responsibilities were diminished. Women discover the same fulfillment through work and professional effort as do men.

Given the differences in the career development cycle, it is interesting to note that women age psychologically in the reverse direction of men. Women at mid-life become more aggressive, more managerial, and less sentimental. They are often entering the work force with a great deal of experience, maturity, assertiveness, and determination. Men at the same age, forty or older, having experienced a mid-life transition differently than women, are becoming less assertive and more sentimental. Husbands tend to become more dependent on their wives and are thinking about tapering off in their work life. Work for women at this time becomes the road to autonomy, independence and a greater sense of fulfillment. "Many women are finding it imperative to attempt to recover those lost capacities, curiosities, fascinations, and abilities that they experienced in younger years, but which were inevitably plowed under in their subsequent culturation as mothers and homemakers."[2] Both men and women thus experience adult career development from a different perspective and yet with many similarities. It is critical that both men and women rediscover and claim the deep spiritual vocational sense of work and the moral imperative that it contains. Neither men nor women abdicate the nurturing homemaking hearth-centered labors that they both share. Some new integration needs to be achieved. Until we work out some new restructuring of the dynamic tension between home and work, only unmarried or childless women are likely to maintain significant careers. Madonna Kolbenschlag gives us a clue when she states: "There are no models in our civilization to inspire this change; it will perhaps be more difficult for men than for women ultimately; we must evolve an ecological model of work, one that sees all functions as equally important in sustaining an equilibrium in society as well as in the personality."[3] Given the complexities of adult life, gender, culture, and natural abilities, what are some of the issues, strengths and guiding factors involved in vocational career development?

Career reflection and reassessment is a normative and optimal experience throughout the adult career development process. Ecclesiastes, the preacher, observed a long time ago: "To everything there is a season, and a time to every purpose under the heavens." Let us look at the seasons and the purpose of these times in the life of adult career development.

1. Late Adolescence

Late adolescence is usually thought of as that time approximately between the ages of sixteen and twenty-two. One of the predominant tasks of this time is leaving the parents' world and beginning to establish, no matter how shaky or how unstable it may be, one's own place in the world. Leaving the family in any form is a major transition from adolescence into the adult world. Up to this time, family life has been central to the world of the individual. In our culture this may continue for some time. This early stage is the first entry into the adult world. Young people at this time often find themselves half in and half out of the family. They are making an effort to separate themselves from the family and to develop some sort of home base. They are seeking to reduce their dependency on family support and seek their own autonomy. For some this is choosing to go away to college. For others it is seeking a job and gathering enough financial resources to move out of the parental home. In our culture, at this time, we are seeing that this late adolescent stage is being extended further and further. Dependency upon parents because of the rising inflationary costs is making it increasingly difficult to become financially independent. One major aspect of the late adolescent stage is moving out of the family home and seeking to become financially independent, establishing new roles and living arrangements in which one is more autonomous and responsible. Going away to college seems to be a natural opportunity to learn these skills. The internal aspects of becoming an adult involve an increase in self-parenting and in beginning the distancing process from the family. These internal processes may begin earlier and extend well beyond the age of twenty-two.

The career development issues at this stage focus around a time of preparation and exploration. It is not uncommon for the late adolescent to become anxious, frustrated, and confused over the selection of a college or the decision not to go to college. The task at this point becomes the selection of either going to school to train for a career or making a living. The importance of this may not be fully understood by the late adolescent since it is very clear that occupational choice and the way that we choose to make a living is a reflection of our total personality. Career choice is not influenced by personality characteristics alone. Chance, economics and culture may also be clear issues in dictating the choice of an occupation. The occupation that is chosen will reflect our personality and play a major part in shaping our personalities in the future. Work provides such things as interpersonal relationships, economic status, social status, and even values that will shape a life-style during the years ahead. Occupations and personality are intricately related. Since late adolescence is a time of exploration, it is a good time for a young person to try many jobs and to explore and test those jobs that seem more fulfilling than others. Not only is it important for the late adolescent to sit down with a career counselor at this time, and to begin to explore with that person both his or her abilities and his or her gifts, he or she also needs to begin to tap into his or her inner value system. It is not too early to begin to explore the vocational questions and to think about God's call. To seek God's guidance from the very beginning is to begin the career development process, knowing that God does have some purpose for us that will be part of God's on-going creative work in this world. A young person may have the inner conviction that doing God's will will be the best route for the future, but be troubled by the question, "What is God's will?"

He or she may marvel at the numerous opportunities and choices of occupations open to him or her and should seek assistance in sorting out the various gifts and skills that he or she has. In late adolescence a person may consider a job that is making a living or select a career. Parents, friends, and others may have some influence at this point, and the process spelled out in the career counseling is critical to understanding a visualized vocation. Certainly on-going prayer, meditation and daily reflection is the way in which we begin to understand God's will for our lives. There is no crystal ball that will predict the one right career. This is the time to explore many options, keeping open to the presence of God's call in life. The important question is, "How can I become a co-creator with God?" Late adolescence is truly the time of openness, idealism, and a willingness to explore new ideas and new concepts, and to find a meaningful and significant purpose in what is being done.

For some, making a living is the direction at this point. In contrast to selecting and preparing for a career, making a living requires that the person acquire sufficient skills and abilities to earn an income to meet the basic needs of life. When the occupation is sought merely for the purpose of making a living, then the task of finding and preparing for the job is generally not very complex, but can be very rewarding and fulfilling.

Both men and women may prefer marriage at this point and join together in a collaborative effort to meet their needs through an occupation or work that involves for them a joint effort in providing sufficient income for the beginning and establishment of a family. If a woman chooses at this time to begin a family, it often means that for a number of years her status and style of life will be highly dependent upon her husband's occupation. We are beginning to see more and more women working before and after marriage, and thus occupational accomplishments and career status become equal in significance to both men and women.

Selecting a career for the late adolescent, particularly in a field that requires long preparation, is considerably more complex than selecting a job for the purpose of earning a livelihood. Preparation may mean going to college and then on to graduate school. It may require going to schools that provide specialized training, thus setting the person in a career track. Since the selecting of a career will in fact affect his or her personality and who he or she becomes, it is assumed that personal goals, values, attitudes, and a sense of God's presence are all involved and wrapped up and expressed in this vocational choice. Late adolescents and adults are not merely selecting a way to make a living but a way of life.

The major task of late adolescence is the mastery of skills, the claiming of independence and the seeking to establish oneself in the adult world. Career counseling from a pastoral perspective would be critical and extremely valuable at this early stage of career selection. It is the time of exploration, preparation and testing. It is therefore a good opportunity to begin on a track that will bring joy and satisfaction over a long period of time. It must also be kept in mind, as will be indicated as we go through the career development process, that the opportunities for change are always available. Naturally in late adolescence movement to another job is relatively easy, particularly in a good labor market. From this possibility can come the sense of drifting and floundering and continued exploration. Career counseling assists the young adult and late adolescent in truly focusing on a more systematic exploration of vocation and identifying the vocational dream.

2. Young Adulthood

Young adulthood is a time of settling down and gaining and increasing the sense of independence. The young adult becomes more self-reliant and seeks to deal with the major developmental tasks of the period which involve assuming responsibilities and duties of an adult member of society. These involve two predominant tasks, intimacy and vocational choice. The acquiring of intimacy and the avoidance of the sense of isolation are tasks that young adults often solve through marriage. Young adults, men and women, begin to experience an intimate relationship with each other and select a member of the opposite sex for the extended intimate relationship of marriage. For those of this age who remain single, they must still in some way or another deal with the issue of intimacy versus isolation and establish an intimate relationship of caring, nurturing and support in some area of their lives.

Part of the independence at this stage is the moving away from the parents and becoming independent and self-reliant. Young adults must test the parental values, messages, expectations, "should and ought" messages, and develop their own values and meaning system. This is a time when the religious values and behavior of parents are questioned and may be rejected, in light of the emerging spiritual and developing value system of their own. Thus the young adult is beginning to establish a niche for himself or herself in the adult world, and this becomes a period of considerable change requiring new adjustments and effective use of both the physical and the psychic resources of the individual.

In addition to the considerable energy devoted to the major task of intimacy and avoiding of a sense of isolation, young adults must settle down into an establishment of an occupation or vocation. The questioning, floundering, drifting, and trials of late adolescence slowly come to an end and the young adult settles down to the mastery of skills and a demonstration of competence in an occupation. In this way, the young adult deals with the inner problems of inadequacy, insecurity and anxiety that are associated with the new responsibilities and new directions in his or her life. Young adulthood then becomes a time of achievement, mastery of tasks and the settling down into the world of intimacy and work.

The achievement of adulthood requires that the young adult begins to study for a career or work that will bring fulfillment and meaning. Since there is no right occupation for a given individual, and each person is capable of being happy and successful in a number of jobs, it is important that the young adult begin to identify and claim his or her dream. It is a time to be sensitive to the inner sense of God's presence, to use gifts, abilities and training in the selection of some vocation that will reflect a response to the call of God. For young adults who have laid a good foundation this time will flow easily, and they will settle into the adult world with confidence and direction. For the young person who has not laid a good foundation for emerging and evolving a career, he or she will continue to flounder or drift, seeking to find the "right" occupation or vocation for him or her. In this continued moving from one job to another, the lack of good experience and good employment record will not look good to employers. It may be difficult for him or her to establish himself or herself in a good career direction. Career counseling is imperative at this stage. This period of establishment becomes for him or her a period of continued upheaval.

Women at this stage may get caught up in the myth that the division of labor is that men should keep themselves busy in the work world and experience the autonomy, independence, and establishment of themselves as an adult there, while women are working while they wait for their real life which is at home and the work of mothering, homemaking, and being the manager of the home. Women at young adulthood may find themselves feeling in conflict and confused about their own goals, caught between work and career and home and family. Some women find that the only way that they can deal with their feelings about being defective in a career and the guilt that may ensue is to try to be a perfect woman, a perfect wife, a perfect mother and a perfect career woman simultaneously, a heavy task for anyone to bear. "Men are more likely to give themselves first to a project, to the choice of work and to their work life. Although a relationship may intervene, they see instinctively that work is the primary and initial means to their identity as men. Women on the other hand put emphasis on relationships. Women bypass or postpone this apprenticeship, to their great detriment. Many women regard their 'work' time before marriage as a waiting period, a kind of limbo before one's real life begins that is the life of relationships."[4] Women in the workplace now represent over forty-five percent of the work force, and the figure is on the rise. This is resulting in a significant population of dual career couples. This pertinent issue will be dealt with in the next chapter. Professional careers and homemaking do not have to be exclusive tasks.

Young adulthood, those years between twenty-two and twenty-eight approximately, is the time of greater independence and the focusing on developing of an intimate relationship and establishment of a vocation. It is the time of getting a vocation, doing a vocation, keeping a vocation and enjoying a vocation.

3. The Thirties Transition

The thirties transition, which is generally between the ages of twenty-eight and thirty-two, is a time of questioning. It is a time of questioning earlier commitments, commitments to marriage, commitments to relationships, family and commitments to a career direction. A reassessment is usually in order and changes may take place.

Transitions are events in which a person experiences a personal discontinuity in life. For the young adult, life has been one which has been inclined to drifting with the tide and applying the rudder rather infrequently. It has been a time of mastery, exploration and seeking to establish oneself as an adult. The thirties transition time invites the person to reassess. He or she develops new assumptions or behavioral responses because the situation is new or requires an inner evaluation of commitments. Transitions may include such issues as relocation, marriage, divorce, unemployment, reassessment of values, and career review. Persons may quite forcefully be asking whether the intimacy or the isolation that they have experienced to this point is meeting their inner sense of meaning and purpose. Some persons who have not established intimacy may be feeling the sense of pressure of the isolation and the aloneness and the desire to enter into a relationship. This may or may not be accomplished as the person moves into the thirties, but the questions are being raised in this thirties transition time. Persons may feel particularly vulnerable at this time and seek to change earlier choices or may continue their earlier choices. This is also an opportunity, a second chance to create a more meaningful and satisfying life structure in both intimacy and vocation. It is a time to be sensitive to the call of God which may now be more clearly heard and experienced based upon the occupational experiences of young adulthood. It is not uncommon for persons to have experienced God's call during the late adolescence period but to have felt that they needed to postpone a response or could not respond to it at that time, only to have the call renewed at this thirties transition. A career change may be in order at this time based upon God's call, self-understanding, known abilities and gifts, and a reawakening of the visualized vocation.

A career change is defined as a change of the person's thoughts, feelings and behaviors that occur over a life span in relationship to the person's work role. Occupation may be changed into a vocation. A shift in career direction may be in order. Career changes may be classified into two categories—those which require a forty-five degree change and those which require a ninety degree change. Some people may even experience a one hundred and twenty degree change in which their career direction is turned totally around and they find themselves going in the opposite direction. For example a person who has been totally involved in a career requiring data gathering and research may realize that he or she needs to make a one hundred and twenty degree turn and become involved in an occupation that has more interaction with people. A forty-five degree change represents those changes that are relatively minor and require little discontinuity with the previous occupation. A ninety degree career change is one that involves major discontinuity with the former occupation. A one hundred and twenty degree occupational change requires a radical shift with major discontinuity with the former career. For example a radical job change is one in which a new job requires neither the training nor the experience demanded by the previous job and is experienced as a total break from the past. To some people this may be in response to their awareness of God's call and their accepting of that call in a vocation that radically shifts them and takes them in an entirely new, meaningful, satisfying and significant direction.

The thirties transition is the time of questioning earlier commitments to marriage, family, relationships, and career, an opportunity for a reappraisal and a second chance to create a more satisfying life structure in both relationships and vocational direction.

4. The Establishment Phase

The establishment phase begins about the age of thirty-two and continues to the age of approximately thirty-nine. It is a time in which roots are being put down and we are dealing with established and establishing lives. Children are growing for those who have them. The developmental shift is from the young adult concerns of intimacy versus isolation to the beginning of the stage of generativity versus self-absorption. This concern will continue for a number of years into middle age. Generativity refers to an individual's concern for others beyond the immediate family, for future generations and for the world in which those generations will live. In this establishment phase, we begin to see the beginning of this. Stagnation refers to the person's becoming and continuing to be egocentric, self-centered, and thus stagnated in his or her relationships to others and to the world community. Since generativity also refers to the concern, establishment and guiding of the next generation, it is appropriate at this time that children are growing and the energy of parents and family is often focused on their training, developing and guidance.

Women at this stage in their lives become particularly aware of the "biological clock." They recognize that time is running out for their biological opportunity to have children. For some who have not been able to develop an intimacy that makes this possible, they begin to experience a sense of tension, anxiety, and at times almost a panicked feeling that diminishes their ability to focus on the high level of achievement in their work. This makes single women particularly vulnerable and married women indecisive regarding whether or not to have another child. Men do not experience this biological clock and therefore may pour themselves into work and to the raising of the family without feeling the pressures and the tensions of time running out.

Both men and women, single and married, should have moved sufficiently away from their parents so that they no longer have to prove themselves to their parents, but are beginning to take a look at who they are and the legacy of should and ought messages passed on to them by their parents. It is not uncommon for adults in this age period to begin blaming their parents for their own personality problems. They reach a point where they must deal with history, how their ego has been shaped and how they take responsibility for their own lives and development. This is a particularly significant time since it initiates the reassessment and reshaping of our egocentricity. It prepares the way for the second half of life in which there is the diminishing of egocentricity and a new alignment for the caring and nurturing of the larger community. Religion and spiritual life are also at an established maintenance phase. Religious beliefs and practices are accepted and repeated without a large number of questions.

It is the time of settling into one's career and a time of no longer trying out various possibilities. The persons accept their choices and buckle down to work. They are interested in establishing their reputation and skills that have been mastered and learned in an earlier time and are now repeated, refined and become quite familiar to them. In many ways the person is settling down and becoming his or her own person.

As a person moves through this stage and begins to approach the age of thirty-nine, questions begin to arise. He or she may think that he or she has reached the peak of his or her capacities in this particular career and begin to ask questions like "Will I have time to do all that I want to do?" There is an acute awareness that time is short and that there is obviously so much to do. Time seems to be running out and the person begins to feel weary about what one is supposed to do and to be. The question again begins to arise: "What do I really want to be?" Changes may already begin to take place in the work area, and some people begin to enhance their jobs through some re-evaluating and reconstructing. When problems with an occupation begin to arise, the young adult flees and seeks another occupation. However, the person around the age of thirty-eight or thirty-nine who is more at home and has more commitments needs to stay, and may find it difficult or impossible to move. Simply redefining the work, redirecting the job, may be helpful at this time. This questioning and beginning pressure begins to push the person into the next stage of mid-life transition.

5. Mid-Life Transition

The middle age transition is a turning point, both a crisis and a dangerous opportunity. It is experienced as a time of change, a period of great upheaval, a time of questioning and particularly a time of reflection on whether earlier dreams and envisioned vocations may or may not have been attained by this time. This transition period is usually around the age of forty, give or take three or four years. It is as though we work and move slowly and carefully to a gate at forty, and with considerable energy, stress and anxiety we open this gate and pass through. It is the passing from young adulthood to middle adulthood. A similar experience happened to us once before at approximately the age of fifteen, give or take two or three years, when with considerable physical and emotional turmoil, anxiety and stress we passed through puberty, leaving childhood and entering into adult life. For this reason, it is easy to see why people would think of the mid-life transition years as a second adolescence. Sociologically, psychologically, and physically change is experienced, and the purpose of this time of life is to help us in reassessing, re-evaluating and redirecting our lives. It is an opportunity to ask the questions: "What have I done with my life? Who am I? What do I want for myself and others? Where am I going? What are my real values? How are my values reflected in my life and my work? What have I done with my early dreams and what can I do with them now?" These questions are accompanied by psychological stress, uncertainty and anxiety. The elements are present for emotional, spiritual, and psychological change.

The mid-life transition can readily be seen as a spiritual turning point. It is the opportunity to again understand, to question the dream and to listen to God's call again. As a person moves through life prior to this time it is uncommon for work to be referred to as "the daily grind," returning to the "salt mines," or the "treadmill," indicating in a very clear way that work by this time may have lost its meaning, its creativity and its connectedness to the purpose of creation set down by God. It is important to be open to God's calling and sensitive to our possible response in vocation. This is a turning point and a transition time not dissimilar to that experienced by the Old Testament patriarch Jacob. He is an archetypal model of the mid-life transition when he wrestles with the angel.[5] He reassesses his life and moves from a self-centered life in which his energy, his time, was directed to mastery and self-centeredness. He begins to realize through the struggle that he must take on a new identity and become a centered self. In the midst of internal and external struggle, conflict, turmoil and wrestling, the opportunity is there to let go of the self-centeredness and move to a centered self.

This mid-life transition is caused by many factors, including physical, psychological and environmental. Some persons are able to gracefully and carefully handle these transitions and move through them into a renewed self. For other persons it may produce a deeply disturbing tailspin, with decisions and changes made rapidly and in the midst of turmoil. Steve, a forty-one year old, told me that at his fortieth birthday party given by his friends and family, he looked around, and it was as if a switch was turned on and he felt anxious, disturbed, concerned and confused. His confusion and the turning off of his love for his wife affected him deeply and eventually ended the marriage. He saw his job as a place where he was trapped. It had been a job that he had enjoyed for almost twenty years, and it was hard for him to see that the job hadn't changed, but he had.

Some of the changes involve a physical change in which the amount of hormones secreted by the endocrine glands changes. These hormones not only affect the energy level and sleep patterns, weight, hair growth, coloration and reproduction capacity of the individual, but are not so dissimilar to the rapid physical changes occurring in adolescence. A person experiencing these bodily changes and possible decline begins to ask about his or her own mortality. He or she is suddenly aware of time running out and the aging process. Men recognize as a man the feminine side of the self, and as women, the more masculine aspects of one's personality. To own the feminine/masculine sides of ourself in a deeper and clearer way results in differing relationships between men and women and an increased value of the feminine aspects by the male and the masculine aspects by the female. This will hopefully allow for men to be more nurturing and caring in their relationships and behaviors and for women to be more assertive and independent in their self-awareness and behavior. Mid-life transition changes in career involve several causes in men and women who are "career oriented," who have spent twenty years predominantly in work. The career related causes for mid-life transition include: (1) the goal gap—the realization that some career goals may not have been achieved and may not be achieved, (2) the dream gap—the discovery that one is not living the visualized, hoped for, dream of young adult life, (3) the step aside gap—that roles and status changes are occurring in work and in the family life and the person is being asked to step aside, (4) the vanity and, for men, virility gap—particularly the fear of loss of attractiveness in appearance and sexual ability, and (5) the meeting mortality gap—and that is recognizing the diminished life expectancy and the coming to grips with one's own death. Time may now be reflected on as how many years do I have left?[6] Critical to our understanding of mid-life transition is the realization that the work does not change, but rather the individual does. Our personality, attitudes, values, relationships, self-esteem and self-understanding begin to shift radically at this time.

Job change and career changes are likely to occur in the mid-life transition. However, Brown notes and reports a study that indicates that sixty percent of the observed changes that occur in mid-life occur within the same occupational category.[7] Persons may stay within their field but make adjustments or changes either into another area or in another slightly different direction, but building upon already established skills. Some persons may make a full one hundred and twenty degree change, and others may simply make a forty-five degree change. The emphasis on the shift from mastery to meaningful work becomes clear when we take a look at salary cuts and salary increases. Many who change jobs take salary cuts to move to a new job, with only eleven percent indicating that salary conditions were important in their careers. Fifty-three percent indicated that the acquisition of a more meaningful job, a more creative and significant one was a reason for a career change, making this the most frequent factor for career change in mid-life.[8] It is clear that job satisfaction, the strengthening of relationships between persons, meaning and creativity become the major motivating forces in mid-life career changes. Persons are now seeking to answer the questions, "What do I really want to do and to be in life?" and "Is what I have been doing for the last twenty years really meaningful, creative, and contributing to the health, welfare, general good of society?" This time raises questions that invite persons to reflect on the meaning of work rather than mastery. Persons begin to question their original goals and what they have achieved at this time. Mid-life transition is truly a time of opportunity in which the person hopefully will make a self-appraisal, a self-assessment, and a re-evaluation of abilities, talents, and gifts. This is the opportunity to integrate the sense of God's call and to move toward vocation. In this way the person captures a spirit of confidence and self-renewal that will support him or her as he or she moves into mature adult life.

Unfortunately, many persons jump impulsively from one situation to another without a systematic assessment or evaluation. It is ridiculous to run away from something without having something to which to run. These persons mistakenly think that the issue and the problem is in the external world of work, of people, of marriage and of children. They fail to take the time to look inward and to deal with the inner upheaval, the inner dreams and the inner tensions. Some make a job change as a way of alleviating anxiety. The anxiety will probably come up at a later time.

Women who are single and who have been involved in a career for twenty years will go through an experience similar to that of their male counterparts. Women who have entered the work force, then dropped out to have children and have been staying home to raise their children, are in a little different predicament. In this latter case the mother is about to lose the children, and at the mid-life transition she may be anticipating the empty nest. For her the intense satisfactions of motherhood are fading. Small children who were totally dependent may have offered enormous satisfactions to her as a mother, and now she may not be able to talk to her son or her daughter who gives her instructions as to how to buy her clothes or drive the car. The mother is about to lose her job. In our society, in the traditional model, a woman who takes on the role of motherhood and homemaking finds that when her children leave at the end of puberty and enter late adolescence, she has in effect discharged her responsibility to society. Unfortunately in our culture, society will make no further demands of mothering and homemaking on this woman. She is also entering a crisis of meaning but from a different perspective. The empty nest looms. It is the time when women begin to think about entering the work force again. Some are able to retool and to re-enter the academic and vocational system. In fact, it is imperative for women to either enter the academic or vocational system or become involved in other meaningful activities in order to overcome the spiritual inertia, the boredom and the sense of uselessness that may occur as their children leave. Claiming a vocation is another way of claiming their own authority, power and identity. This may mean claiming and using effectively their own masculine side. At the age of forty to forty-five a woman is still young enough to start a career, to re-enter an old one, or to devote her time to new interests or a new vocation.

Many middle-aged women are pushed into the work force as a result of the need to supplement the family's income or to help finance a college education for their children. Mid-life transition for them is similar to repeating the late adolescent stage as they seek to develop skills, note their abilities and enter again into the adult world of work, competition and the marketplace. It is extremely important that they not sell themselves short or enter into an occupation which is demeaning or below their abilities, skills, gifts, talents, or training simply for the sake of "working." It is extremely important at this time that women therefore take the time to reflect, to meditate, and to pray and seek to understand God's call for them at this time in their lives. They can then respond in vocation even if it means re-tooling and re-education. Women who combine marriage and career will not be faced with the same adjustment problem as women who have put their careers on hold while entering into the world of motherhood and homemaking.

Thus the mid-life transition is a time of opportunity, a time of radical life-style changes. Some may enter these changes without adequate preparation or forethought, but they know that there must be something else to life. They seek some greater sense of meaning, purpose and creativity, something more that brings and moves them toward a greater sense of self-actualization. Those who are able to recognize that this is a personal, internal, emotional, spiritual and attitudinal opportunity will be prepared. They will use the resources of forethought and adequate assessment to change. They may change their vocation. Mid-life is a unique spiritual opportunity to respond to God's call in vocation.

6. Restabilization Phase

The mid-life transition phase is followed by a restabilization phase which begins at approximately age forty-four and continues to approximately age fifty. The opportunities and the reassessment made during the mid-life transition stage begin now to bear fruit. Those who have gone through it with some stamina, stick-to-itiveness and self-reflection begin to move into this phase with a sense of a feeling of being settled and moving again, whereas for those who have gone into a deep tailspin, it is an opportunity to move more slowly and reflectively and to re-establish the harmony and balance necessary for moving through the rest of mid-life into mature adulthood. These persons may experience a sense of stagnation at this time and begin to move from one job to another, seeking to gain independence, a sense of self-worth or self-esteem and a new direction. They may be considered the adult dropouts. Not that they drop out of school, nor did they terminate their employment, but rather they have become stagnated. They are experiencing what Erik Erikson refers to as self-absorption. They become absorbed in their own problems, their own failures, and begin to project onto jobs, family and others the reasons why they have not been "successful." Such persons have the sense of standing still and accomplishing little while they watch others rising to new heights or achievement and moving toward a time in which their careers peak and they experience great joy, meaning and satisfaction in their vocation. Those in such a tailspin may find it difficult to pull out. Once they do, they can begin the process of restabilization. They can settle in and raise meaningful questions, moving them through the solutions regarding their own meaning in life, career and life-style.

For those who have successfully navigated the waters of the mid-life transition and are involved in the restabilization, they experience a time which is busy and a period of continual questioning. Yet because of their focusing, it becomes a time of bearing fruit. Certainly this is the period when children begin to leave the nest and parents begin to reflect. They may question and regret errors that have been made in child-raising. They may be faced at the other end of the scale with having to take care of their aging parents who now require and demand a lot more of their attention, time, funds and energy.

These middle years are busy years, and the problems that are faced are many. The major characteristic of this restabilization phase is that of increased intrapersonal focus. Any change in career, whether it be a forty-five degree change or one hundred and twenty degree change, will be related to the increased concern and search for the restabilization of identity, intimacy and trust. Both men and women will be working on these issues. For men, it is the reinvestment in a vocation seeking new meaning, direction and self-actualization. Women who have stayed in the career force will also be working on these issues. Women who may have focused on the internal work of home and motherhood are now more focused on the world outside the home and in developing their desire for identity, authority, intimacy and trust in their own awareness of abilities and being. These forces alone may be the driving forces that motivate men and women to make career changes. These career changes are related to their new view of life. Careers blossom, and along with the new energy and restabilization, the training, experience and abilities previously mastered are now combined with a new sense of meaning and purpose that bears fruit during this time. Persons may have increased energy to try even to climb the ladder a little further or to bring meaning or direction to their current position.

It is not uncommon for persons in mature adulthood to experience the pressure of more aggressive and imaginative younger associates working hard for advancement. Some people may feel at this point intimidated by youth. However, when they are able to focus in on their strengths and abilities they are able to blossom. Persons at this stage are usually doing their work not so much from the sense of obligation but are beginning to experience a new sense of love and commitment to what they are doing.

Carl Jung viewed middle age as a watershed. The first half of life is spent in preparation for living, the second half in experiencing meaning and purpose and in preparation for old age.[8] The restabilization and the bearing fruit in this stage is often revolving around the realization of God's presence in the world, that God does call us. The call that may have been experienced from God as young adult or in our late adolescence or even in the thirties transition may now be experienced differently. We are called to become attuned to God both in our lives and in our work and now move from simply occupation into true vocation. If this has not occurred before this time, then God invites us to respond in vocation. Since we are now moving into the re-establishment stage of meaning and the combining of abilities with meaning, our life-style changes and we become more aware of the inner desire to become attuned, for wholeness, and our journey toward self-actualization. Work is not a reason for living, nor should living be a reason for work. Rather work becomes a vocation that brings deep satisfaction, joy, and a co-creative nature. For some, work may become simply putting in time so that they have the money to do what they really want to do. Work can become something that we love and experience as a significantly integrated part of our life, a vocation. The stagnation experienced in the late thirties either happily or unhappily has by this time given way to new directions, to new meaning, to a re-establishment and stabilization in our vocation.

7. Renewal

The restabilization phase now becomes a time of renewal, of enjoyment, of acceptance, and of excitement in personal and professional life. These are the years beginning at approximately age fifty and continuing through sixty-five. It is the time that teenagers refer to as the establishment. It is very clear that middle-aged people run the world and someone has to be the establishment. In our society each middle generation in its turn is obligated to accept this responsibility of being the establishment and running the world. There is no better time than this, since both men and women by the age of fifty and beyond have negotiated the rapids in the rivers and pushed open the transitional doors and successfully integrated both mastery and meaning into a renewed sense of purpose and attunement with God. This is truly the age of generativity. Time can now be spent on attending to more of the inner development issues and reflection on the meaning of life and the mentoring of the young. This period from approximately fifty to sixty-five is the longest phase in career development and personal growth, and has within it many variations, opportunities, and areas of stress. Generally it is a time of relative calm, acceptance and enjoyment of life. Certainly it is not without its areas of questions, problems and issues.

The mature years are productive years, and what persons may lack in power, speed and glamor, they make up in experience, wisdom and maturity. These mature adults have a number of things going for them and against them. Experience is the most valuable asset—experience in ego integration and a new alignment with the self which brings an emotional integrity and a spiritual richness as the basis for new life structuring and thus a new source of energy. The energy is now revolving around meaning and the embracing of self-actualization. The experience that is such a valuable asset may in turn become a liability as persons in mature years experience certain levels of rigidity. Flexibility of mind, body and spirit is the goal throughout life. Mature years are more susceptible to rigidity. When this is embraced and hardness is permitted, then experience becomes an enemy. Wisdom and maturity are indeed assets which come with mature adulthood and help persons become productive. The wisdom and maturity permits a responsive rather than a reactive behavior, a manifestation of concern for personal relationships and a sensitivity to persons. People have worked out by the latter part of mature adult life many of the problems of life and have developed a satisfactory approach to life, a sense of meaning and an organizing life principle. These concepts are reflected in Erikson's understanding of the latter part of mature adult life as integrity versus despair. Those who embrace despair as they move into their sixties find themselves looking upon life and reflecting back on a series of missed opportunities and missed directions. They often project onto others their problems and blame others for their sense of despair in not having succeeded in bringing meaning and self-actualization to their lives. Boredom may set in as persons repeat the same patterns or procedures. They may fail to energize or bring any creativity to what they are doing. Risk taking seems less likely to occur during the latter part of the mature years. For those who are willing to risk, for those who are willing to innovate, the years become a continuing process of renewed creativity.

Reality, job age and biological age do not always match calendar age. Some may feel young and vibrant at the calendar age of sixty, while others feel tired and obsessed with health and become involved in real or imagined obstacles. The result is that they slow down until they eventually coast into boredom.

Health certainly is an issue for the mature adult. There are concerns about their physical energy and strength which may be declining. Men in their fifties are susceptible to heart problems more so than women. They may become very conscious of this or of the slow diminishing of their physical strength. As the mature years progress there is a slow reorientation toward retirement, and the concerns begin to mount regarding the financial conditions and what retirement will be like. In our current society we are beginning to see companies offering persons early retirement at the age of sixty, fifty-five, or sometimes even earlier. This most certainly becomes a time of career assessment, re-evaluation and reorientation to a second career. We'll look at this in more detail in the next section.

Certainly this renewal stage is a stage of deceleration with the approach of retirement. There is the slowing of the pace of work and the reducing of the time and energy expended in work. Persons may cling very tightly to work as an indicator of their sense of role and identity. They may refuse to delegate or to refocus tasks on others through nurturing and mentoring new persons coming along. For others they realize that they have no need to control others or to drive themselves so much. They can then be in touch with their inner self. They can claim who they are and manifest a concern for warm, personal relationships and enjoy watching others grow, assisting them and directing them so that they in turn may take their place on the career ladder.

The renewal years are also times of spiritual questioning, growing, renewing and engaging in conversation of a spiritual nature. There is a great deal of potential for growth and spiritual depth, the opportunity for deep commitment to becoming co-creators with God. As a person approaches retirement, then the question again arises regarding a sense of vocation and a new awareness of God's call at this stage of life.

8. Retirement

The retirement stage is usually referred to as that time in which a person terminates his or her major career track and may stop work entirely or shift to a new vocation. As life is extended and retirement is not mandatory, this time becomes truly the golden years of modern maturity, a time of continued commitment to usefulness to society and growth for oneself. As people continue to live longer the issues of what to do after "retirement" become more critical.

For some retirement is the end. They see it as being put out to pasture. They see it as loss of identity as if who they are is what they do. Men in particular, who have spent all their waking hours focused around work, and who suddenly are told that they are now retired and do not have to come into work, may find themselves going into a depression as they experience a powerful and often negative grief process. This negative attitude makes retirement painful, boring and stagnating.

For others, retirement is a great career. When a person retires, he or she does not suddenly change just because he or she retired. He or she doesn't suddenly give up his or her talents, gifts, abilities, knowledge, skills and experience. Rather he or she is given more choice and more opportunity than he or she ever had before. Certainly the choices represent some apprehension. People begin to redesign their lives to experience a greater sense of balance between such issues as work, learning and leisure. Prior to retirement work probably claimed the bulk of time, and leisure and learning took up less. With retirement, work may not need to claim as much time, but leisure and learning may. Retirement requires that a person look at the balance or imbalance of work, learning and leisure in his or her life and adjust these three elements into a satisfactory harmony and balance. Working in a career is a choice that is *now* possible. In a recent article by Carolyn Burd in *Modern Maturity* (February–March 1988), retired persons indicate that they want a job that adds zest to their life because it's fun to do or it takes them places or they feel satisfied and appreciated in it. They want work simply because there's something that these retired persons know how to do and they want to share it with another. They want work that is fun, with no time clock, work that is with people, and that challenges them to be alive, vital, and to use their skills and knowledge in either a similar or another field. Work that was high on the list was consulting, teaching, writing, and travel. These sound like ways that the retired person will be able to pass along whatever he or she knows to others. In doing this he or she is indicating the desire to be involved, to be respected and to have his or her years of knowledge and experience appreciated and absorbed by younger generations. The sense of identity, intimacy, and trust continues to be present. To be whatever you want to be sounds wonderful, but may at the same time be so overwhelming that it prevents the retired person from moving in any direction. Some people find that it is necessary to work after retirement simply to maintain themselves financially because of the lower pay that was earned before retirement and social security benefits just do not help them to meet their needs. The second benefit of working is personal benefit to remain productive, to help others, to pass on one's knowledge, and to offer a chance to interact with others and share with people. Many employers are willing to offer retired persons flex time so that they can come and go as needed. A new type of work on a new schedule is a good way for the retired person to ward off boredom and rigidity, the two enemies to flexibility and experience. It is extremely important for the retired person to live in the present and not in the past. If one concentrates on the past, one won't enjoy the present. One can become obsessed and pained about the past or live in it with joy, but it is the present and the future that is important.

God's call continues whether one is retired or not. There are many people who in retirement experience and know God's call, have redirected their lives, and personify God's love and co-creation in a dynamic, moving way. One cannot help but be moved by the work of Mother Teresa or the life of Gandhi. A positive attitude and enjoying life makes it possible for a retired person to consider finding work as a vocation.

Chapter 6

The Dual Career Family

Both men and women are involved in the work force in the United States. According to the Occupational Outlook Quarterly of the U.S. Department of Labor, Bureau of Labor Statistics, Fall 1987, women will have a larger share of the labor force by the year 2000. The number of women in the labor force will rise from fifty-two million in 1988 to sixty-six million by the year 2000. The number of women will rise twice as fast as the number of men because the proportion of women who participate in the labor force will continue to rise. In 1987 sixty percent of all the women in the work force were married. This number will also increase at the same rate and the same proportion as women in the work force in general. With the increase of married women in the work force, we see the rise of the phenomenon of the dual career family. A dual career family denotes the type of a family structure in which the husband and the wife pursue active careers and a family life simultaneously. This is in contrast to the traditional family where the two principal actors, husband and wife, divide their roles in the traditional way, with the husband as the sole breadwinner and the wife as the homemaker. In contrast the dual career family has a husband and wife, each of whom has a vested interest and deep commitment to his or her own career as well as the family. Both spouses are committed to a successful career and also desire to lead a family life and be happy as marital partners.

It is helpful to note that there are several variations of the dual career family. The first one is called the dual earning couple. In the dual earning couple, two people work at an occupation to earn money and are married to each other. They seek both a happy marital relationship and work. The second is the dual career couple. This is a couple who have moved from simply being involved in work to claiming a career. For the dual career couple the emphasis tends to be on career as a primary source of personal fulfillment. Third is the dual earning family. In this type the spouses with children work at a job in order to provide the family income. The family usually grows out of the couple relationship and is denoted by the involvement of children. Fourth is the dual career family. This variation emphasizes both career as a primary source of personal fulfillment and the raising, nurturing and parenting of children as a primary source of personal fulfillment. These several variations constitute what used to be a non-traditional family or couple relationship. It is in fact becoming the norm. The dual career phenomenon is here to stay and is on the rise. The number of dual career couples has increased from 900,000 in 1960 to 3.3 million in 1983, an increase of 267 percent over a twenty-three year period.[1] I will use the concept of a dual career family as it symbolizes the final evolution of the other three. Thus the dual earning couple may become the dual career couple and the dual career couple may be transformed into the dual career family. Certainly each aspect of the dual career couple, the dual career family or the dual earning family or couple has its unique and its individual aspects.

The persons in the dual career family operate in a very delicate, inter-dependent balance. Each person seeks to juggle and to balance the many aspects in which he or she is involved: career, household responsibilities, personal and private world. These worlds are not segregated or compartmentalized units in the individuals' lives but overlap and to a substantial degree affect the balance of the system. The systems that support the dual career family style are intricately interwoven. An analogy could be made between the dual career family and a hanging mobile. If one part of the mobile hanging in space is removed, the other parts become unbalanced and tangled. Removing or adjusting one piece of the mobile or adding another piece to the mobile requires that each other piece be adjusted accordingly and the system must respond to the changes. In the mobile many options exist as to which particular piece is lengthened or shortened and how much, or whether a piece is added or subtracted. The point is that dual career families must find the correct harmony and balance in this delicate, interdependent relationship that brings satisfaction to each of the parts. The dual career family as a hanging mobile is affected by such things as promotions that might require a move, a new child, the upgrading of one's formal education, the loss of a job, etc. With each new shift, the total system must be adjusted accordingly. This makes the dual career life-style a much more complex and challenging style than other ventures that the average individual undertakes. The couple and the family must work in some kind of harmony and balance to maximize the aspects of life that bring optimism and satisfaction in both work and in the home. This becomes a formidable, challenging task, a task that can bring both rewards as well as a complicated dilemma.

I will look at the various factors that occur as the dual career couple moves through different phases to identify the dilemmas and the strengths of this dual career phenomenon. The developmental phases to consider are: first, the career-marriage decision phase, second, the career-marriage commitment phase, third, the dual career couple phase, fourth, the dual career family phase, and, fifth, the dual career couple phase revisited.

Career-Marriage Decision Phase

This phase is characterized by the self-assessment process in which individuals, male and female, must take a close look at their own beliefs, values, feelings, needs, goals and interests and see how these will mesh in both a career and a marriage. Both tasks, those of selecting and deciding on a career and of choosing a mate, are part of the young adult developmental tasks spoken of in a previous chapter. Questions in this phase really revolve around how my career decision, training, education, and opportunities to work in many fields will affect me as a man or as a woman if I decide to get married. Will that marriage be a traditional one or a non-traditional one? Since the questions of choosing a vocation and choosing a mate are extremely important decisions, they must be considered very carefully in terms of their impact both on the career and on the couple relationship.

Men and women who reach the young adult decision stage of career-marriage come to it with different developmental and personal attitudes, perspectives and values. Women grow up putting greater emphasis upon relationships and connectedness, while men grow up putting greater emphasis on competition and mastery of skills in tasks. Carol Gilligan in her book *In a Different Voice* gives us helpful insight into these developmental differences. Women are never disconnected from important others. They stress relationships in which there is caring for others and strong commitment to human relationships. Men, on the other hand, develop a detached, idealistic, competitive stance, for the most part minimizing relationships and emphasizing the successful completion of a project. Therefore men are more likely to give themselves first to their work and the project, to the choice of work and the mastery of the tasks needed to move into a career. Relationships are important to men; however, men instinctively assume that work is a primary and initial means of identity. Men in our culture seem to have been given a very strong message that they are what they do. It is expected that they should work. This understanding is deeply ingrained in the Judeo-Christian tradition from the time of the Adam and Eve story. Women may also consider work to be extremely important in the sense of who they are and their identity. However, more important is the other dimension of connectedness, relationships, and the cultural directive to be involved in home and parenting. Many women regard work time before marriage as a waiting period, a kind of limbo before one's real life begins, the life of relationship, marriage and children. Women who resolve to work and move into a career through training need to have a clear understanding of the place of their career in relationship to homemaking and parenting. The priority that women place on considering relationships as primary in their decision making helps us to understand and explain the difference in sequence from men and women in career development. The sequence for women is usually partial education, marriage, children, a job, more education, and a career. This is a fairly common pattern for women. Men, on the other hand, usually go through education and into a career to which they commit themselves over a longer period of time, perhaps making several shifts and retraining several times. The differing sets of values that women and men bring to the decision of career affect their view of themselves and the kind of marriage-career decisions they will make. It is clear that the rising aspirations of women coupled with greater educational and career opportunities and the current economic conditions point to an ever increasing number of persons who will move into a dual career couple relationship.

This first phase is then the time for men and women to seriously think and consider whether they seek a traditional marriage or a non-traditional marriage involving dual career.

Career-Marriage Commitment Phase

This phase is the decision to commit oneself to both an enriching, satisfying and loving marriage and a satisfying, successful career. Persons having made the choice to enter into a dual career couple relationship are usually proud of their life-style and seek at the same time for models that will give them innovative techniques of coping with the exciting but highly demanding and tension provoking facets of their new life together. The couple have now moved from the talking, thinking and speculative stage into the practical day-to-day beginning of a marriage, caring for and dealing with early marital issues, at the same time seeking to balance career and the demands that are made there. Couples who have decided to get married and enter into this commitment to both career and marriage have a number of questions on which they must now focus. They may be in the early stage of both seeking jobs and needing to develop a job seeking strategy. If both partners are still seeking a job, do they want to look for jobs in the same or in different organizations? It would be hoped that they would look for a job in the same geographical area. The question that will begin to arise is: Whose job takes priority? If one person is invited to move to another location to secure a job, to further his or her prospects, what does that mean to the other spouse's current occupation and career development?

Growth in a marriage and a career in a dual career couple is possible when each person enters into that relationship as a whole person. Often people enter into a marriage thinking that they will become whole by marrying the other person and thus complementing or filling in the side or part of themselves that they have not fully developed. In such a marital relationship, dependency is fostered and an over–under relationship develops with each person taking on the opposite role. Seeking to maintain such a complementary relationship may cause difficulty in the future. Those persons who enter into the marriage and commit themselves as whole persons accepted and loved for who they are, accepting and loving who they are, enter with a balance of autonomy and homonymy with each other as two whole persons. Together they seek to bring into being an interdependent marriage, a two way covenant that respects, accepts, and values the gifts and talents of each partner. In such a relationship marital satisfaction can grow when both partners work outside the home. Being working husbands and working wives does not create marital discord. A career adds another dimension—which could be positive and/or negative. Naturally there will be some tension and stress in the early months of marriage adjusting to the new life. This stress and anxiety is normal and is a natural by-product of the adjustment period each couple has to accomplish. During this time a balance of commitment to both marriage and career can be worked out.

For the dual career couple, the career and marriage are both experienced as vocational responses to God's call. Each partner is free to grow and move toward self-actualization both at work and in the couple relationship. Commitment is the major factor for dual career couples as they face career and marriage. Marital satisfaction comes out of a sense of personal freedom and support that can be present in the dual career couple. Growth for this couple comes from the affirmation, acceptance, and claiming of one's strengths as well as one's own pain and feelings of hurt and the willingness to accept and understand the pains and hurts of the partner. When this is possible they can seek creative alternatives.

Dual career couples must take responsibility for the choice of their life-style. They have decided to balance three full-time jobs: her career, his career, and their career which involves the household chores, the enhancement and growth of the marriage and the day-to-day tasks of living as partners. The day-to-day tasks of household chores are a thankless job. Household chores are work that is unvalued. How these get done will be critical to the dual career couple. For generations it was women who did "the dirty work" and took care of the three c's of cooking, cleaning and childcare. When a woman adds to this a fourth "c" of career, the dirty work takes a lower priority. The three c's must now become the province of both husband and wife. Women who resolve to work in their careers must also resolve not to leave home without enlisting another, their spouse particularly, in the care of that home and share in an equal way the "c's" of cooking, and cleaning, and, later on, childcare. The division of household labor is the only solution. Dual career couples need to learn early a spirit of cooperation. This is not an easy task, given the lack of models and the cultural injunctions that have stressed household chores as woman's work and work outside the home as a male priority. If this issue is not dealt with and resolved in the early years of the marriage-career commitment, then the couple that is involved in dual careers may find themselves later on facing a career-marital duel. The couple at this phase commit to each other, to communicate, to resolve problems, hurts and pains by respecting each other's autonomy needs and inner sense of God's calling. When this happens it will strengthen the career-marital commitment.

Dual Career Couple Phase: Getting Established

After this commitment is made to being a dual career couple, it is followed by a longer phase of seeking to establish the norms and rules by which this dual career marriage will work. The couple may have gotten married based on the fact that they "love each other," but couples quickly realize that marriage is not built on that love but rather on the acceptance and the negotiation that occurs between the two of them that makes it possible for love to grow and be experienced as a vital and integrated part of their relationship. For the dual career couple this is particularly important because of their intense commitment not only to each other but to their work. This is a time when couples establish their initial modes of behavior, contracts and patterns upon which the marriage and the career will grow. Patterns dealing with who does what around the house, the cooking, the cleaning, the laundry, the mowing, the vacuuming, the car washing, the paying of the bills, must all be reevaluated, considered and discussed because of the couple's seeking to establish a new type of relationship based not on the old traditions, but on some new models. If they are also to succeed in work, then they must contract together and discuss the priorities that each puts on work, including travel time, time away, moving because of job promotions, or change, and work that may be brought home. This is the time for the couple to begin practicing and testing solutions to both the stress and the joys of being a dual career couple. Pure and simply, work overload faces married couples and could turn dual careers into dueling events.

Clearly stress is built up around the allocation of tasks and the division of labor in the house and the sharing of home management responsibilities. Couples are caught in a role and identity overload. The dilemma is that two roles are expected—first, their job at the workplace; second, keeping the home in order. Since both spouses work outside the home, this leaves the question of the division of labor in the house and the management responsibilities to be worked out. The first thing that couples must work on is not simply the delegation of the tasks, but the recognition that the household tasks are related deeply and clearly to gender based roles, identities and values which have been passed on and internalized by them early in life.

Dual career couples do not have many models to look back on that will assist them in this dilemma. Within the last fifteen years we have seen more and more dual career couples and will see this mode of marriage and career relationships increasing as the years pass. This generation is in the middle, caught between traditional role models, gender expectations, values and the desire to develop non-traditional new models called dual career couples. The traditional roles passed on to us are that men busy themselves in the work of the world, developing their autonomous, independent and assertive side. Women busy themselves with relationships, become the anchor and manager of the home, developing their supportive, dependent and non-assertive side. In this traditional model women engage in the outside world vicariously. Dual career couples face this gender role issue head-on and affirm that both men and women can busy themselves in a career and be autonomous, independent, and assertive. Both men and women can anchor themselves in relationships, manage the home and be supportive, dependent, and focus on the home.

This new model of an egalitarian relationship must be claimed. However, it faces a multitude of forces that seek to maintain the traditional gender roles. The husband is still identified with the breadwinner role and wives continue to be identified in the homemaker role. The culture as an unspoken force tends to support this traditional pattern of behavior, emphasizing the wife's place in the home and the husband's place in work. Institutions, business, government, education and religion may hire women and see women in the workplace each day, but still, on some deep, unconscious traditional level, expect them to be predominantly the homemaker. An article by Eleanor Grant in the January 1988 *Psychology Today* entitled "The Housework Gap" reports that although most men say that husbands should do more housework when their wives have a career, in practice they just don't. Wives spend considerably more time doing housework than do husbands, almost thirty hours per week or seventy-nine percent of the time devoted to such chores. Husbands do about four to six hours each week, about fourteen percent of the chores. When both spouses are employed full-time, the wives do less of the housework, about seventy percent. Full-time homemakers complete about eighty-eight percent of the household chores. Household chores continue to be "women's work."

In the dual career marriage it is clear that men spend more time developing their work role. Women are expected not only to develop their work role but to maintain the household chores and responsibilities. They have two full-time jobs. Many women experience a great deal of frustration and even a decrease in their mental health. This comes from being unable to commit themselves to their careers as fully as they would like.

There is a difference in the quality of life experienced by husbands and wives in the dual career family. Professional wives in general experience lower levels of mental health, that is, feelings of well-being, than their husbands. This is because they experience more frustration in simultaneously pursuing careers and maintaining homes and children.[2]

Dual career couples need to understand and recognize this pervasive non-verbalized gender-oriented traditional view of work and home. There are couples who are able to talk about this and to deal with it in a more creative way. They seek solutions. Above all they must deal with the continually present anxiety and tension that they are pioneers and new role models for an egalitarian understanding of work and home. The community, the business world, and even the church do not give couples much assistance or support in this task. In this establishment stage each couple must first begin by dealing with their own understanding and clear verbalization of the roles of husbands and of wives. They must not only verbalize but consciously and unconsciously support each other's desire for an egalitarian relationship, a balance between the workplace and the tasks and chores of homemaking.

The frustration is that even though husbands and wives may perceive their careers to be equally important and see their work and family world in more or less the same way, they will encounter impediments, frustrations, and resistance to this view from the culture. Unfortunately, the traditional model lives underground. Women, for instance, may experience in the workplace impediments to experiencing high levels of satisfaction and enjoyment or a sense of well-being in a job well done through blocks in promotion and negative attitudes, fears and anxiety. Hopefully this is changing in the workplace. As men and women become more aware of new roles and new models, then solutions that involve a balancing of roles and demands both at the workplace and at home will occur. This will happen through the juggling of responsibilities and tasks, careful planning of career change, transition time, the division of labor in the house, and the sharing of management responsibilities. Truly the egalitarian model of dual career relationship will be possible.

As husbands and wives are able to commit themselves fully to their careers, to their couple relationship, and home management, stresses may build up over competitive feelings. Competitive feelings surface in the dual career couple if one partner gets an edge over the other in terms of career progress. Since the individuals are not necessarily equal in their abilities, their talents, or their intelligence, it is quite possible that in these first few years one partner may advance more than the other in his or her career, and feelings of competition and even envy may surface as a result. When competition is present in the relationship and it is not admitted and identified, then it goes underground and comes out in envy, anger, and career dueling. Healthy competition energizes people and could very well increase the successful productivity of each person. However, excessive competition can be unhealthy and dysfunctional in the dual career marriage. It is in these times that the strength of the marriage, the ability to communicate and resolve problems is put to the test. This can be worked out when couples are committed to each other and able to resolve their problems with some creativity and admit their anger and their competitive feelings. When this happens, competition does become energizing. However, when the competition is used to put the other down or is seen as threatening the ego or the person's sense of self-worth, then it becomes unhealthy. The couple may need assistance in dealing with the tensions and the underlying feelings, attitudes and values that make competition a dysfunctional factor. For example, given the underlying traditional models of marriage, the most common mechanism that wives adopt to cope with competitive feelings in their husbands is to reject promotions and to try not to be too successful. They tend to keep a careful watch on how far they go in their careers so that they do not outstrip their husbands and thus arouse strong competitive feelings. This is a natural stand for most women who have been taught that relationships are most important and for most men who have been raised in a situation that stresses competition and success as related to self-worth. Not to deal with the competitive feelings openly and to communicate directly about them is in fact to force them underground and to cause the couple considerable problems, including resentment and anger, and puts the dual career couple into a dueling relationship.

There are a number of couples who work in the same area of expertise. They may have met and married while in a specialized graduate program or professional school. They share common interests, common goals, and a common value system. Thus we see couples working together in such fields as law, medicine, teaching, and ministry. They get married not only for better and for worse, in sickness and in health, but also to become a team in work and employment. They often seek to support one another in their common career commitment. This couple must deal openly and directly with competitive feelings and convert those feelings into a cooperative relationship. The cooperative model invites persons to work side by side at work and at home. For generations couples have worked side by side on the farm or in small family shops or businesses. Now we are seeing more and more professional couples working shoulder to shoulder in medical centers, churches, research labs and the classroom. These couples seek to integrate their activities both at the workplace and at home.

When both partners work in the same area of expertise, they may find that this is both a strength and a problem. Time together may be time to share but may also become time when they only talk about work; they then see the world from only one focus and have a limited perspective. Their circle of friends may remain within their small professional grouping. A clear dilemma that these couples face is that they may not be able to find jobs in the same location. They may not have opportunities to work together. If one of them finds a job, will the other also? Their desire to work as a team in a cooperative dual career may not be possible because of the job market. Some couples who seek employment together as a team may find that together they take a reduced compensation since the employer is hiring them as a team and not as two individuals. This may work to their advantage or cause them to feel resentful and have problems.

This establishment phase then seeks to establish the dual career couple as a meeting of the minds as to how, and in what way, this dual career relationship of both full-time commitment to work and full-time commitment to the relationship will be established. How much time will be devoted to work and career and how much time will be devoted to each other? How much time will be devoted to personal activities and how much time will be devoted to career activities? The task of the couple is to accomplish this new model and establish it on a firm base with two-way communication, developing open expression of expectations and supportive behavior.

The Dual Career Family Phase

This is the time when children arrive and the family expands, whether planned or unplanned. The shift from dual career couple to dual career family is probably the most stressful period in the life of the dual career couple, especially if there is more than one young child in the family. The predominant issue for the couple now becomes time—time for work and career development, time for the already established household management needs, time for the self, and time for the children and family development. The couple must talk. What is going to be the role of each of them in the child rearing? Fathers who delegate all the child care to the mother forsake their child and abandon their responsibilities as fathers. Children have the right to have both a mother and father, though both these persons may be pursuing their own careers. Therefore the couple as the heads of the household must seek to plan together the necessary adjustments and accommodations to make this life-style work, a life-style which is very complex and multifaceted. Children do need a great deal of time and attention. Time becomes that scarce commodity for everyone.

It is at this point that the traditional family model of the husband focusing on work and the mother focusing on the home and the raising of the children will be most apparent. This is a real issue both consciously and subconsciously for mother and father. It is at this point that the mother is likely to experience extreme role overload. There may be expectations that she is responsible for the child rearing and care. She may modify her work schedule and work commitments until the children are grown up. If this is not done, many mothers feel guilty about not giving enough time and attention to their children. What often happens is that when a mother working full-time and a father working full-time are confronted by illness or a problem with one or more of their children, it is the mother who usually adjusts her schedule to take care of the family or child's problem. Part of this is encouraged through the culture and the embedded values that mothers should be over-involved with child raising, permitting fathers to be under-involved with child raising. If mothers get caught in this guilt trap, then it is highly likely that they will become overwhelmed by the many role expectations that are placed on them.

One way that mothers resolve this issue is by putting their career on hold and spending a number of years raising particularly their small children. This time period may be anywhere from two years to ten years and puts the career of the mother on hold. It means that at a later date she may or may not be able to re-enter her career choice at the level at which she left. The result, of course, is that the husband usually progresses and advances as do many other men. Women find themselves playing catch-up. As long as the society and the cultural values see child raising and household chores as the primary responsibility of mothers and women, mothers will allow the spillover from family and the demands of the children to interrupt, forego, or delay their career development. The point is not that mothers are to be sympathized with and husbands are to be derided, but rather that dual career families need to find reasonable, meaningful and satisfying models by which the dual career commitment, the couple commitment and the family commitment can all be balanced. This requires couples to find new and creative solutions. They must sort out and spread out the routine dirty work. Joyful parenting requires both, since it is this third job, home, parenting and marriage, that is the most complex. Some couples find that contracting out the "dirty work" is the solution. When husband and wife agree and support one another in the contracting out of the larger cleaning tasks, then the mutually agreed upon house jobs can be shared among all the family members. Even the contracting of routine responsibilities to extended family members, child care centers, helps.

If the dual career family is to maintain itself, spouses must support each other in their commitment and determination to stay married, to stay as a family, and to stay in their respective careers. This is not an easy task, but a possible one. Perhaps one of the important things to note is that skills are transferable. That is, skills used on the job that assist individuals in making good decisions, planning, managing large financial budgets and doing significant management tasks can be transferred to assist the couple in sorting out the issues, the problems, and finding solutions. A myriad of solutions are possible when the couple uses their talents, gifts and abilities in a committed two-way communicating relationship. Family problems may not be much different than work problems and may be assisted by the same type of problem solving, goal setting and strategies used by the person in the career. This is possible when we begin to understand the emotional and psychological overload and baggage that are often carried into the marriage and can prevent a powerful effective executive from using those skills and gifts in a home.

Dual Couple Phase Revisited

This last phase is the time of the empty nest. It is again the time when the couple, having raised their children and launched them into their own careers and marriages, are now again a dual career couple. This time brings with it a new sense of freedom, time, opportunities, and a chance to further both the couple relationship and the career relationship. The children have grown up and left home, and the couple experiences the freedom to handle their work and nonwork lives in any way they choose.

This is often the time when couples rediscover the spiritual sense of work relationship and the moral imperative that it contains. The imperative is to nurture health centered vocation, integration of achievements and world shaping enterprises that have generally been avoided. For the dual career couple to reach this phase means that they have developed an egalitarian, cooperative sense of both vocation and family. They have dealt with a number of stressful and painful internal and external pressures. It is these couples that will become the models for younger couples just entering the dual career world. Ultimately, we must evolve an ecological model of work that sees all functions as equally important in sustaining an equilibrium in society as well as in the personality. As dual career couples and families become the norm, it will become more and more imperative that we support their efforts. They will show society new models.

Drawbacks and Benefits of the Dual Career Life-Style

The dual career life style has been identified as a very stressful one that is establishing new models and setting new values in the male-female relationship both in the couple relationship and in the career. It is natural that the persons seeking to maintain this very delicate mobile balancing act should experience in their relationship and in their career commitment both drawbacks and benefits.

Drawbacks

The dual career life style has drawbacks. It is a non-traditional model often filled with stress. Each partner seeks to mobilize his or her strengths to handle the stress, the major drawback of the dual career life-style. Seven major drawbacks are experienced.

The first drawback to the dual career life-style is lack of time. Couples are naturally trying to balance couple time, family time, self time and the major time commitments involved in a vocation. The result is a lack of time to do any one of these things adequately. Some part gets short-changed. Often it is the self time or the couple time, which in turn makes it difficult for the couple to maintain their relationship through good communication, sharing and enjoying the intimacy and the commitment of their marriage. There is never enough time at the end of the day for all the tasks and expectations that couples try to put into that day. Couples often report that they experience themselves on a merry-go-round going at a rapid pace trying to keep together both themselves and their families and to find enough time for meaningful and satisfactory experiences in both home and work. No matter what we do, time marches on. It is a commodity that cannot be changed, a limited resource. How we choose to use our time is our responsibility. For the dual career couple, it often seems that everyone else is demanding their time and in charge of their time.

The second drawback of the dual career life-style is that of fatigue and stress. Demands and expectations produce fatigue and stress. People become exhausted and experience an emotional overload with all that is expected. Certainly, this fatigue and stress may be related to unrealistic expectations; however, there is so much to do and so many people depending upon each couple that the unrealistic expectations seem like real ones, especially if the person has received a message that he or she should be responsible and be a superman or a superwoman. Spouses of a dual career couple may come home tired, exhausted and stressed from their work only to find that there is a large amount of work still to be done at home. Part of the fatigue may be related to the resentments that build up because of the demands that other people make upon their time. There is no time for relaxation and rejuvenation except perhaps during planned or designated vacations. Simply maintaining the dual career life-style means that stress occurs.

The third drawback of a dual career life-style is children. Many couples feel that their life is not complete unless they have children. When children enter the life of the dual career couple, the demands, the time commitments, the stress and the fatigue multiply. Children need, require and should have nurturing, present parents. Since this ideal is not possible, the children are often seen in a dual career life-style as a burden, an interruption, and a problem. This is particularly noticeable when one of the parents is expected because of work demands to spend days or weeks away from the home, leaving the full responsibility of parenting, homemaking, and career to the other spouse. Children magnify the stress, fatigue, and time dilemma on the dual career family, especially during the early years. The addition of children symbolizes the dilemma for the dual career life-style. Parenting itself is a full-time vocation, worthy of the attention of both husband and wife. When a couple waits to have children for a long period after they are married, the dual career life-style of the couple is often quite rigid and set. Introduction of a child is seen both as a blessing and a dilemma. It means a radical change in that life-style, some anxieties, guilt, fatigue, pressures, and indeed the stress of trying now to add a fourth full-time vocation to three already full-time vocations.

The fourth drawback of the dual career life style is the stress involved in the household chores, the third job which has to be maintained. Unless a couple has carefully worked out a structure and a life-style that permits a full share of this third job, it becomes an additional burden, usually for the wife. She may begin to resent this and feel angry with all the household chores that "fall to her." The maintenance tasks of the household are endless, repetitious and unrewarding.

The fifth drawback of the dual career life-style is that work often intrudes into personal and marital relationships. Keeping work and personal/marital relationships separate is not an easy task, especially if the spouses are in similar occupations. Work can permeate everything. It can take over conversations and time spent at home, and no energy is left to think about anything else. Many dual career couples who work in the same field feel that they are never away from their vocation because they find themselves talking about it all the time. When couples do not have clear boundaries, then the work spills over. It is particularly stressful when both couples work in the same office, in the same location, next to each other, and thus see each other all the time. Not only will work spill over into personal/marital relationships but often the marital relationships and personal needs will spill over into the work situation.

The sixth drawback of the dual career life-style is that it places limitations on career growth and choices. Career decisions must be discussed between the couples before changes in work, in geography, in schedule or in tasks can be accomplished. Whose career should take precedence may become the issue. Where to locate and where to live may become the issue. If a couple find themselves linked in their career, then one may feel guilty if he or she progresses faster than the other or one's growth may be dependent on the abilities and skills of the other. Since both are committed to a full-time career, certainly the location and the choice of location where they can work becomes in itself limited.

The seventh drawback and dilemma for the dual career life-style is that there are no previous generational models. We are experiencing the first generation of a new non-traditional life style. Therefore, spouses have no frame of reference, history or traditional models to look back to or to learn from in resolving the stresses, dilemmas and issues of being a dual career couple. They are truly the pioneers who will set the models for future generations to follow. This in itself is stressful and yet at the same time a tremendous opportunity to find new solutions to new problems.

Benefits

One might wonder why couples would opt for a dual career life-style, given the many dilemmas, stresses, strains and drawbacks that each couple and family must face. Actually some of the stresses, drawbacks and dilemmas noted may be for some couples the very strengths that make the dual career life style attractive and rewarding. There are in fact numerous rewards as well. The rewards of being in a dual career life-style may more than compensate for the drawbacks experienced by each spouse.

The first major benefit of the dual career life-style is that there are two incomes. This may make it possible for the couple to live at a higher standard of living, to develop a cash reserve, and to enjoy vacations, a nicer home, dinner out and some of the more expensive things in life because they are both bringing in a paycheck. For other couples, the second income becomes a necessity to maintain a standard of living for their family that they expect. Some dual career life-styles do not begin until the need arises when children go to college. Then a spouse may return to work or begin an occupation with the initial goal of a second income to support the college education and spiraling costs of living and maintaining the household and relationship at a certain level. The couple have more disposable income, which may in fact meet their security needs, safety needs and self-actualization needs.

The dual career life-style secondly allows self-fulfillment for both spouses. Being involved in the career brings a high level of self-esteem, accomplishment, power, and ego-strength in the accomplishment and growth of the work side of the personality. Since a person's needs cannot be totally met in a one-to-one marital couple relationship, many needs can be met by adding to that couple relationship the career. It does allow each partner to develop and grow personally, professionally, and in their marital relationship.

The third benefit of a dual career life-style is that it increases the appreciation and respect that each has for the other. Maintaining a dual career relationship requires a high level of both autonomy and homonymy. Each person in his or her own right has gifts and talents that he or she uses in his or her career which forces both spouses to stretch intellectually, personally, and professionally, thus increasing the appreciation and the respect that each has for the other and the joy that each can feel in the accomplishment of the other.

Having a wider circle of friends is indeed a fourth benefit gained from the dual career life-style. Each spouse not only has the friends they share but has friends, colleagues and co-workers in his or her career, thus broadening and enriching his or her support system, network and friendships. When this is shared one with the other, it enriches and strengthens them as a dual career couple and brings to them a broader perspective and appreciation for the world.

The fifth benefit of the dual career life-style is that it makes a marriage more interesting. Each couple is confronted with and invited to develop an egalitarian role model to deal with competition and cooperation and use the resources of time and talent in a more deliberately planned and intentional way. The marriage is enhanced by the richness of the understanding that each brings, for each knows what it is to live both in the world of work and in the world of marital relationship. The marriage is certainly enriched and enhanced when each couple can accept the other and support the other in who he or she is and what he or she does.

The sixth benefit of the dual career life-style is that of children and the benefit of shared parenting. When both spouses are committed to the career and to their parenting role, then they must work out a mutual egalitarian parenting with shared responsibility that brings joy to each person. Children in turn get to experience both sides of the male and female parenting. The roles that are presented are ones of cooperation and sharing. Children are also invited to grow by taking on increased responsibility. They grow and take their part in this cooperative dual career family.

Dual career families and life-style presents a positive role model for children. It presents a role model of intentional relationships, of facing issues together, of supporting one another in a collegial depth understanding. They experience the sense of stimulation and the energy that comes from the dual career life-style and begin to be aware of both the need for tasks and flexibility in the family. The model of shared breadwinner and shared parenting will be a model for the children that they will understand, modify, and enhance as their generation moves into a dual career life-style.

The final benefit of the dual career life-style is that it is establishing a new model for generations to come. As couples together face new challenges from time to time, they enhance their sense of self-esteem, self-worth, and gain a greater sense of importance and power both in the family and in their careers. They can become involved, cooperatively, equally, in the issues, stresses and joys that make a dual career life-style workable. Both husbands and wives in this dual career life-style experience a sense of collegiality, an awareness that together they can face the issues, and deal with them in a creative, positive manner. "The level of overall satisfaction experienced by the dual career family members in the various facets of their life, work, family, and personal spheres, keeps them in good physical and mental health and enables them to function effectively in life."[3]

Essential Qualities of Dual Career Families

Dual career families are here to stay and need all the help they can get in making it a positive, self-actualizing experience and model. Sekaran in her book *Dual-Career Families* states that several specific dynamics will help the couple to experience a good quality of life as a dual career family. They are:

1. Mutual love, understanding, and respect for each other as two individuals who have their own needs, aspirations, and goals even as they both share marital life with joint needs, aspirations, and dreams. Spouses know what they want and pursue their goals unfettered by normative or environmentally set expectations.
2. A healthy team spirit that allows both to collaborate emotionally and professionally with a strong sense of togetherness. Competition gives way to joint problem-solving and cooperation.
3. Flexibility and a willingness to adjust to the needs of the situation rather than being unyielding and rigid about pre-determined modes of behavior.
4. A sense of fair play and equity to ensure that it is not only one partner who practices flexibility or has power but both. Androgynous values help here.
5. A continuing redefinition of what success means to the couple. This will require that both partners be sensitive to each other, to the needs of the family, to the needs of each other and to the needs of the relationship, and jointly they define what success means.
6. The maturity to realize when to act independently and when to act in a dependent mode, and when to be interdependent.
7. The need to develop and continually work at communication and listening skills to ensure that small issues do not snowball into big ones. Every couple needs to know how to communicate

their needs to the other, and how to resolve problems in a creative, effective manner.
8. The need to manage time effectively and build structures to make the transition between home and work a smooth one.
9. The strong commitment of each partner to the relationship and a high level of motivation to make the success of this complex dual career life-style. They must choose it again and again.
10. A spiritual life that invites God's presence into the midst of the marriage, their work and their family through continued meditation, prayer and the sharing of mutual affirmations, forgiveness, and love.

The dual career life-styles will be successful and will continue to grow in numbers in our society. Couples will need to have a clear sense of who they are and agree on where they are heading. If God is a part of the relationship and calling each to vocation, then they can sort out many of the anticipated and unanticipated problems that will inevitably arise from time to time. They will develop a health-giving dual career life-style.

Notes

Chapter 1

1. John O. Nelson, *Work and Vocation* (New York: Harper and Brothers, Publishers, 1954), pp. 19f.
2. Marsha Sinetar, *Do What You Love—The Money Will Follow* (New York: Paulist Press, 1987), p. 8.
3. Louise Welsh Schrank, *Lifeplan* (Illinois: VGM Career Horizons, 1985), p. 2.
4. Erik Erikson, *Identity and the Life Cycle* (New York: International University Press, 1959), pp. 50f.
5. Duane Brown, Linda Brooks and Associates, *Career Choice and Development* (San Francisco: Jossey-Bass Publishers, 1984), pp. 169f.
6. *Ibid.*, pp. 192f.
7. Virginia Satir, *Peoplemaking* (Palo Alto: Science and Behavior Books, Inc., 1972).
8. Gen 25:23.
9. Gen 25:26.
10. Gen 25:27–28.
11. Elizabeth B. Yost and M. Anne Corbishley, *Career Counseling* (San Francisco: Jossey-Bass Publishers, 1987), p. 19.
12. Gen 27:1–45.
13. Eric Fromm, *Psychoanalysis and Religion* (New Haven: Yale University Press, 1950), p. 97.
14. Sinetar, *op. cit.*, p. 32.
15. Sheldon B. Kopp, *If You Meet the Buddah on the Road, Kill Him!* (Palo Alto: Science and Behavior Books, Inc., 1972), p. 107.
16. Sinetar, *op. cit.*, p. 144.
17. *Ibid.*, p. 191.
18. Brown, Brooks and Associates, *op. cit.*, pp. 31f.

145

146   Choosing Your Career, Finding Your Vocation

19. *Ibid.*, pp. 61f.
20. Yost and Corbishley, *op. cit.*, p. 14.
21. Carl Robers, *On Becoming a Person* (Boston: Houghton Mifflin Co., 1961), p. 35.
22. Howard Clinebell, Jr., and Harvey Seifort, *Personal Growth and Social Change* (Philadelphia: The Westminster Press, 1969), p. 64.

Chapter 2

1. In the theory of C.G. Jung an archetype is an inherited idea or model of thought, derived from the experience of the race, and presented in the unconscious of the individual, controlling his or her ways of perceiving the world. See C.G. Jung, *Analytical Psychology* (New York: Vintage Book, 1968), pp. 40f.
2. Carl Michalson, *Faith for Personal Crises* (Nashville: Abingdon Press, 1958), p. 103.
3. Dorothee Soelle, *To Work and To Love* (Philadelphia: Fortress Press, 1984), p. 60.
4. *Ibid.*
5. *The Interpreter's Bible*, Vol. I (New York: Abingdon Press, 1960), pp. 511f.
6. Evelyn Whitehead, *Seasons of Strength* (New York: Image Books, 1986), p. 23.
7. *Ibid.*, p. 24.
8. *Ibid.*
9. Daniel D. Williams, *The Ministry and the Care of Souls* (New York: Harper and Brothers, 1961), pp. 101f.
10. John Sanford, *The Man Who Wrestled With God* (New York: Paulist Press, 1987), p. 93.
11. *Ibid.*
12. *Ibid.*
13. Whitehead, *op. cit.*, p. 35.
14. Elmer G. Million, *Your Faith and Your Life Work* (New York: Friendship Press, 1960), p. 43.
15. Michalson, *op. cit.*, p. 113.
16. *Ibid.*
17. *Ibid.*, p. 198.
18. *Ibid.*, p. 111.
19. Soelle, *op. cit.*, p. 41.

20. H. Richard Niebuhr, *The Purpose of the Church and Its Mission* (New York: Harper and Brothers, 1959), p. 64.
21. Whitehead, *op. cit.*, p. 9.
22. Martin Buber, *I and Thou* (Edinburgh: T & T Clarke, 1937), p. 39.
23. John Sanford, *Dreams, God's Forgotten Language* (Philadelphia: J.B. Lippincott Co., 1968).

Chapter 3

1. Duane Brown, Linda Brooks and Associates, *Career Choice and Development* (San Francisco: Jossey-Bass Publishers, 1984), pp. 31f.
2. Thomas E. Brown, *Inventory of Meaningful Ability* (Unpublished Worksheets, 1969).

Chapter 4

1. Elizabeth B. Yost and M. Anne Corbishley, *Career Counseling* (San Francisco: Jossey-Bass Publishers, 1987), p. 131.
2. *Ibid.*, p. 132.
3. Morgan, *Use of Inner Experience*, p. 136.
4. Betty Edwards, *Drawing on the Right Side of the Brain* (Los Angeles: J.P. Tarcher, Inc., 1979), pp. 26f.
5. Louise Welsh Schrank, *Lifeplan* (Illinois: VGM Career Horizons, 1985), p. 138.
6. Yost, *op. cit.*, p. 202.
7. Schrank, *op. cit.*, p. 158.
8. *Ibid.*, p. 165.

Chapter 5

1. Madonna Kolbenschlag, *Kiss Sleeping Beauty Goodbye* (New York: Bantam Books, 1981), p. 67.
2. *Ibid.*, p. 80.
3. *Ibid.*, p. 81.
4. *Ibid.*, p. 73.
5. Gen 32:22-32.
6. William Van Hoose and Maureen R. Worth, *Adulthood in the Life Cycle* (Iowa: WmD. Brown C. Publ. 1982), p. 45.

148　*Choosing Your Career, Finding Your Vocation*

7. Duane Brown, Linda Brooks and Assoc., *Career Choice and Development* (San Francisco: Jossey-Bass Publ., 1984), p. 378.
8. *Ibid.*, p. 380.

Chapter 6

1. Uma Sekaran, *Dual-Career Families* (San Francisco: Jossey-Bass Publ., 1986), p. 9.
2. *Ibid.*, p. 45.
3. *Ibid.*